The History of Schenectady, NY Coloring Book

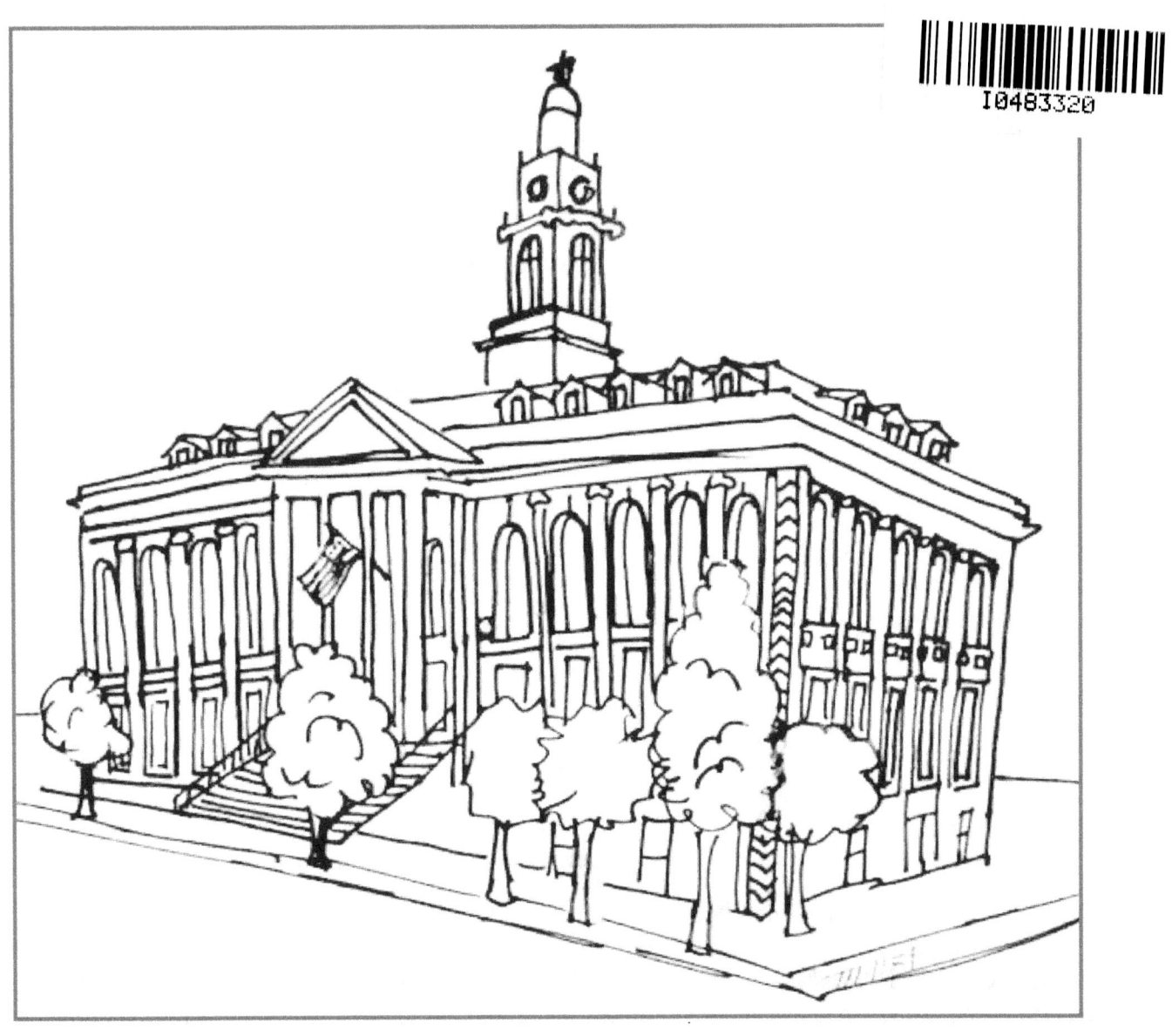

By Mary Frances Millet

ISBN: 978-1-64184-268-6

NOTT STREET OFFICE

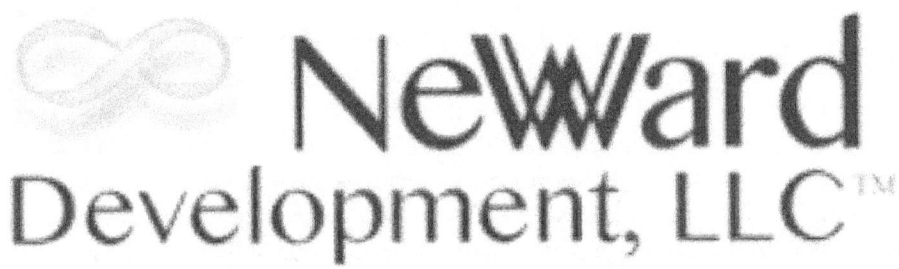

NeWWard
Development, LLC™

Renttropolis
Online Property Management Software

K

IMAGE & DESIGN
www.kaimageanddesign.com

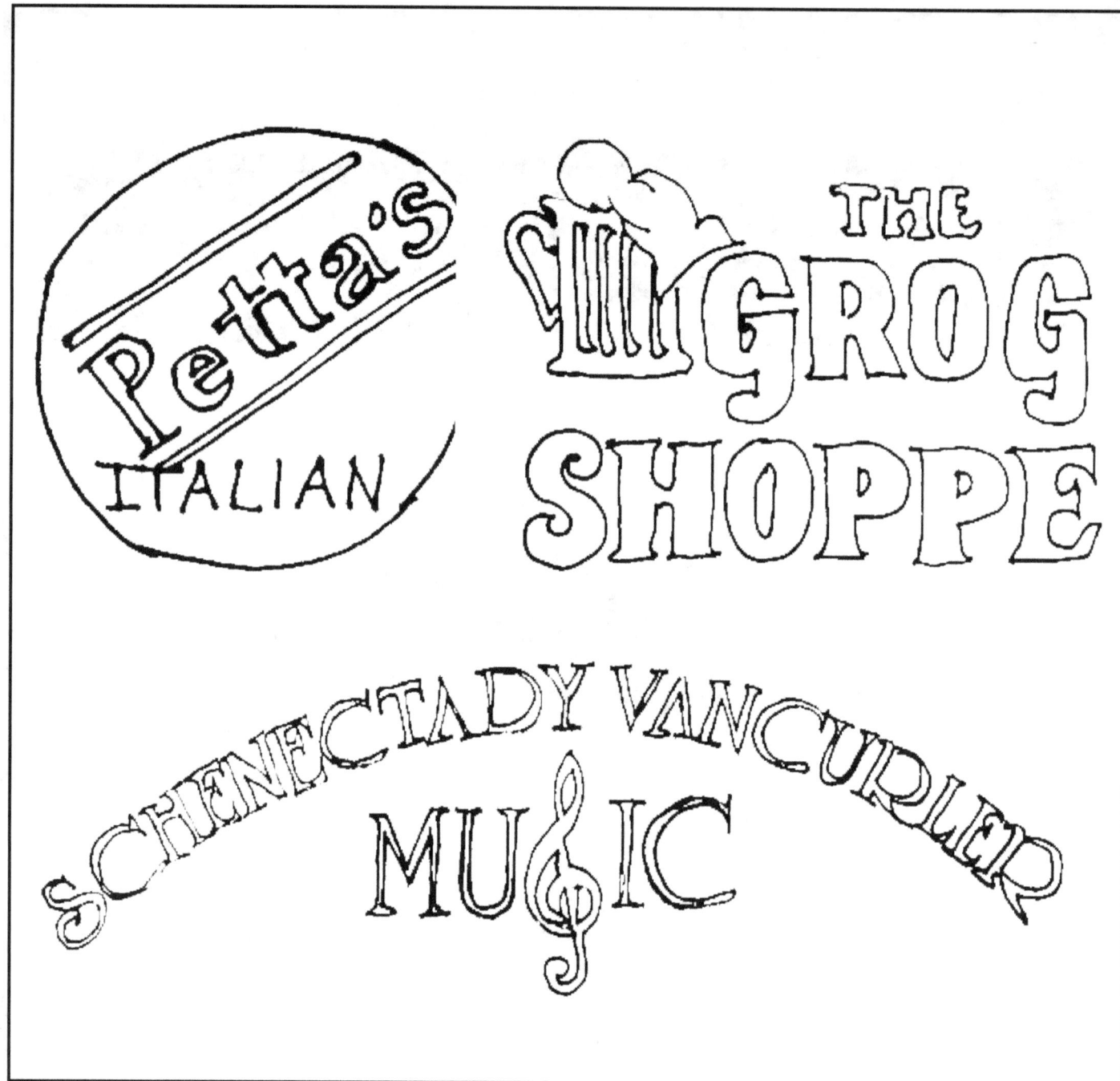

Gone But Not Forgotten Dept.

The Grog Shoppe, closed this year was a rustic mélange of beers and burgers. It was in business on Erie Blvd since 1925, when the Erie Canal was filled in.

Pettas Restaurant is gone now but who could forget that sauce. Open for 65 years, it will now serve a church community.

Van Curler Music was THE place for sheet music and was conveniently housed in Proctor's famous Arcade. (a must see in itself)

I hope you enjoyed this book as much as I enjoyed creating it. Calendars, mugs and notecards of these illustrations will be available soon. Please email me at maryfrancesmillet511@gmail.com for information!

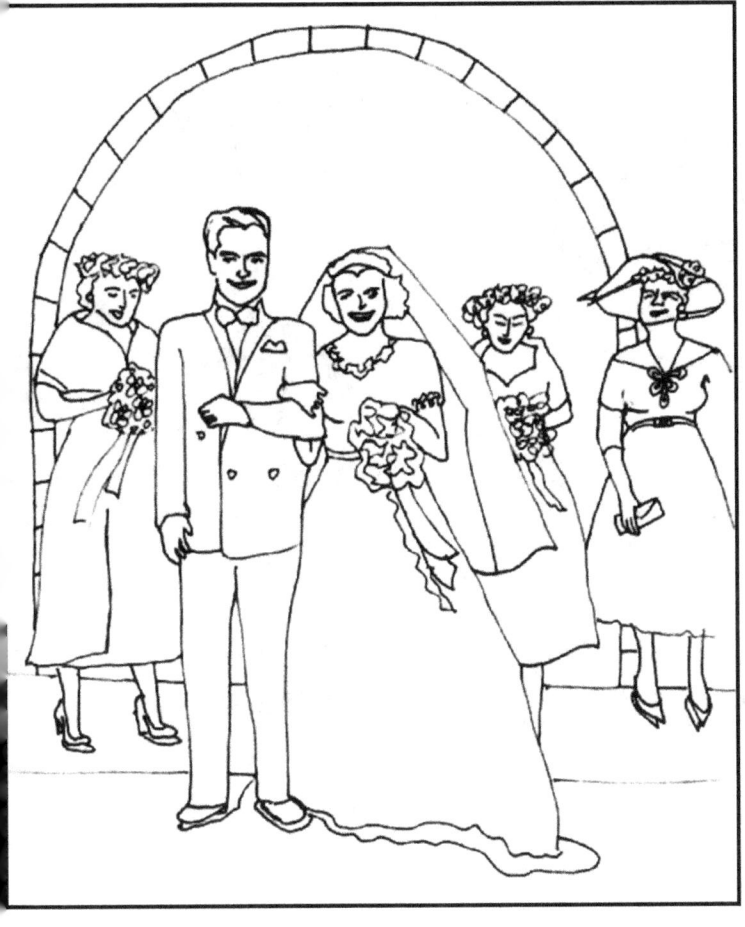

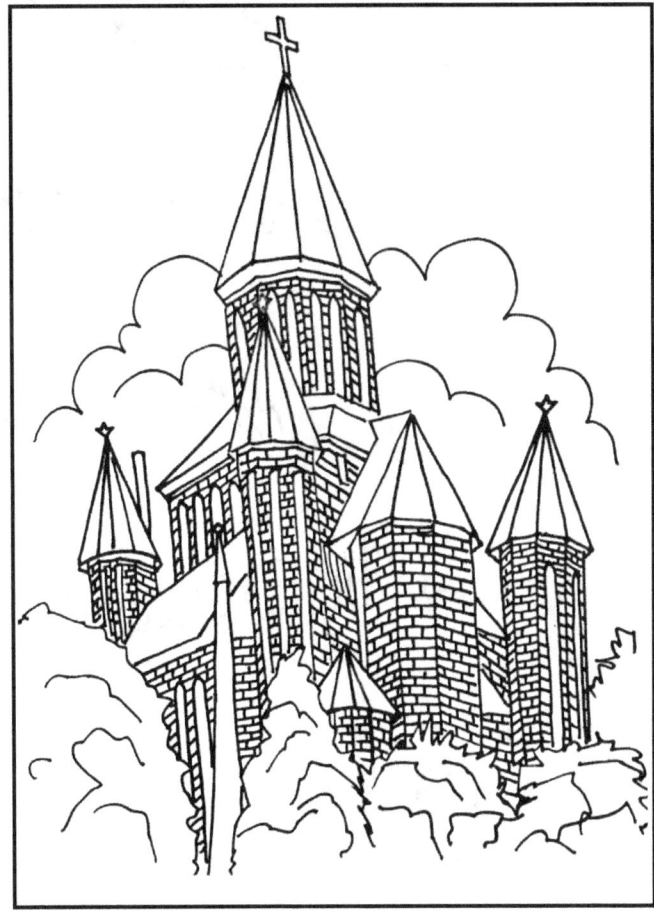

This coloring book is dedicated to my mom and dad, Jeanne and Bob Millet, pictured above on their wedding day, July 21, 1951 at St. John the Evangelist, whose loving care and support kept my artistic talent flourishing and gave me the honor of being born in this great town.

St John's was built from 1892-1904 and is one of the grandest churches in Schenectady. Its magnificent brick exterior with its 230 ft steel/glass spire and 14 ft high gilded iron cross foreshadows the awe-inspiring interior featuring 1,700 - seat oak pews, a Carrera marble altar, windows from the Royal Bavarian Art Institute in Munich and 536 stone and stained glass angels looking down on you in adoration.

This coloring book's illustrations are completely hand drawn. Thanks to many people who provided both financial and emotional support, without whom this book would not have been possible. Special thanks to Jim Gleason, Carol Deyoe, Peggy Gray, Christine Firth, Susan Gatta Stoyan, Angela Kaufman, Carol Barre, Sandra Collins, Shannon Speicher-Allitt, Margaret Fisher, Mary Ann Van Alstyne, Kimberly Huhn, Jane Morrison, Mary Sieder, Heather Hutchison, Rebecca Shattuck, Lorraine Westervelt, First National Bank of Scotia and Jessica Roberts.

Thanks to Kerry Endres of K A Image & Design, graphic designer extraordinaire, Greg Solomon of Nott Street Office for the printing and First National Bank of Scotia for underwriting the printing.

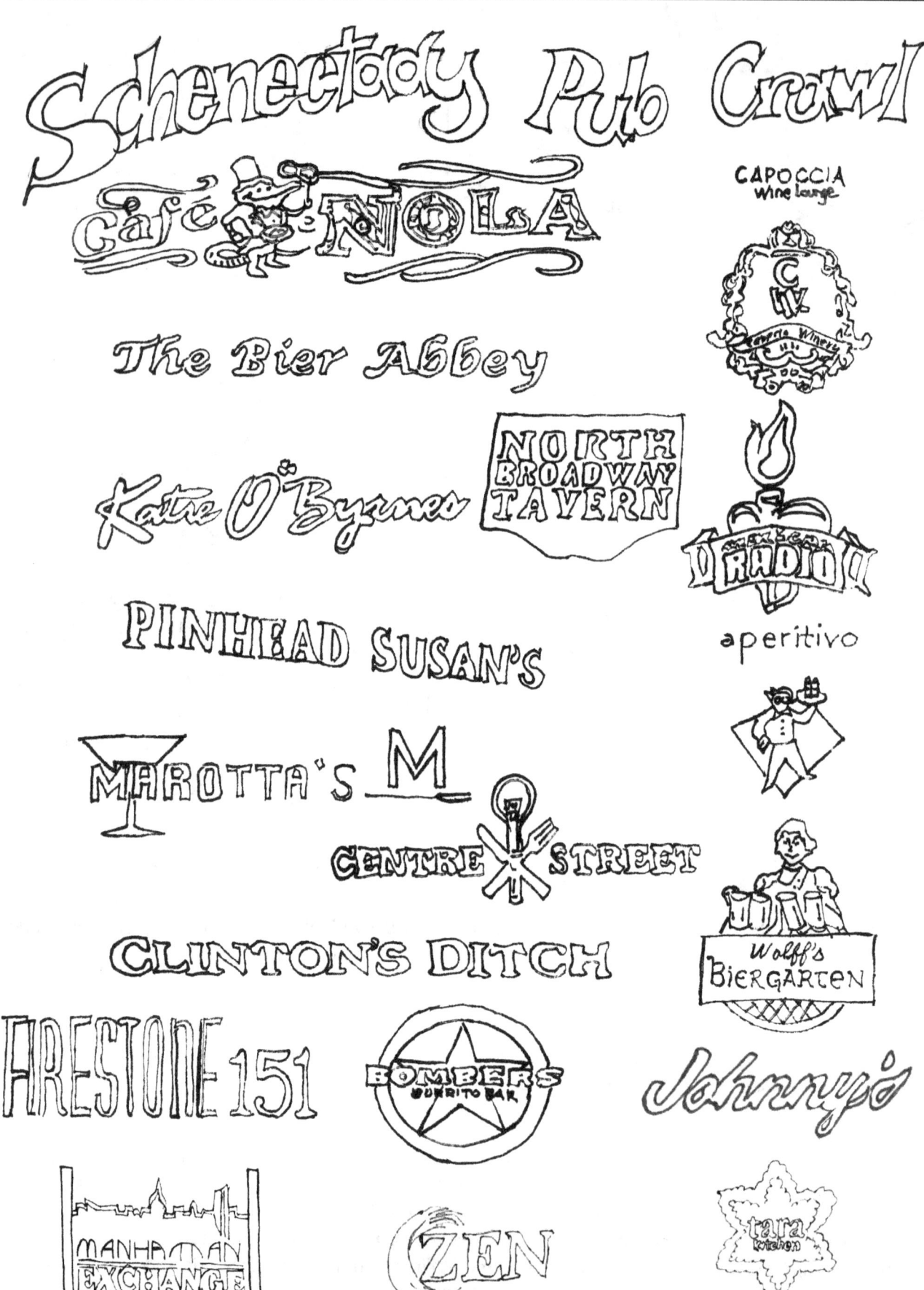

Pub Crawling around downtown Schenectady

Foreword

Schenectady's name was anglicized from the indigenous people's language meaning "beyond the pine plains." Located on the Mohawk River-Great Lakes corridor, it had an important influence on the development of the frontier through the Erie Canal. Schenectady was the transfer point for resources between the east and the undeveloped west.

Colonial Schenectady was a cultural microcosm and foreshadowed much of what America was to become. Like many towns in the new country, it was a melting pot of people of different cultures who combined their commercial prowess. The Dutch were the first settlers who were entrepreneurs in fur trading. French, Scots, Irish, Germans, Italians and many more contributed their own particular brand of commerce.

Many inventions and "firsts" came out of this town as you will see.

I have enjoyed both drawing and researching images for this book. I spoke to many business owners to get their permission to include them and was given many stories about this town. I am grateful to have received a lot of images and information from the books of Larry Hart, past historian of Schenectady, Historical Society and Chris Hunter of MiSci.

I have also eaten at many of the restaurants that are illustrated here (in the name of research of course) and I have to say, this is a foodie's heaven. From diners and pubs to upscale gourmet restaurants and bars, I couldn't choose my favorite because they're all so good. A hot dog at Newest Lunch is a great old school experience as is an elegantly presented meal at the Glen Sanders Mansion. There's something for every taste here in 11 square miles. New ones keep popping up too.

A 90 year old friend told me the Klondike Tower was built by the WPA. Since it was the government and took so long, they nicknamed the WPA "We Poke Along." Another 89 year old friend told me of climbing up the back of the American theater stairs because they could not pay for tickets. She told me "Schenectady had 6 theaters and was THE testing ground for the talking pictures and if you couldn't make it here, you couldn't make it anywhere."

I am a third generation Schenectady native. I had an idyllic childhood growing up on Washington Ave. in Scotia, running around Collins Park, reading at the Abraham Glen Library or eating ice cream at Jumpin Jacks under the light of the giant GE logo shimmering off the Mohawk River like the moon. We took the bus to downtown to shop at the stores, played in Central Park, had Sunday dinners at Kelly's, visited family at their grand home on Lenox Rd, attended kids' parties at the Hibernian Hall and ate a lot of Freihofer's goods and Perreca's bread. We now take our kids to the Central Park hill in the winter and slide right down to the frozen Iroquois Pond..

My maternal grandparents, Sylvester (Gus) and Regina (Landry) ran the Roosevelt Hotel where the Armory now stands. My parents, now passed, lived here and my family and I still live here.

My paternal grandparents, Bill and Barbara (Schaf) also lived here.

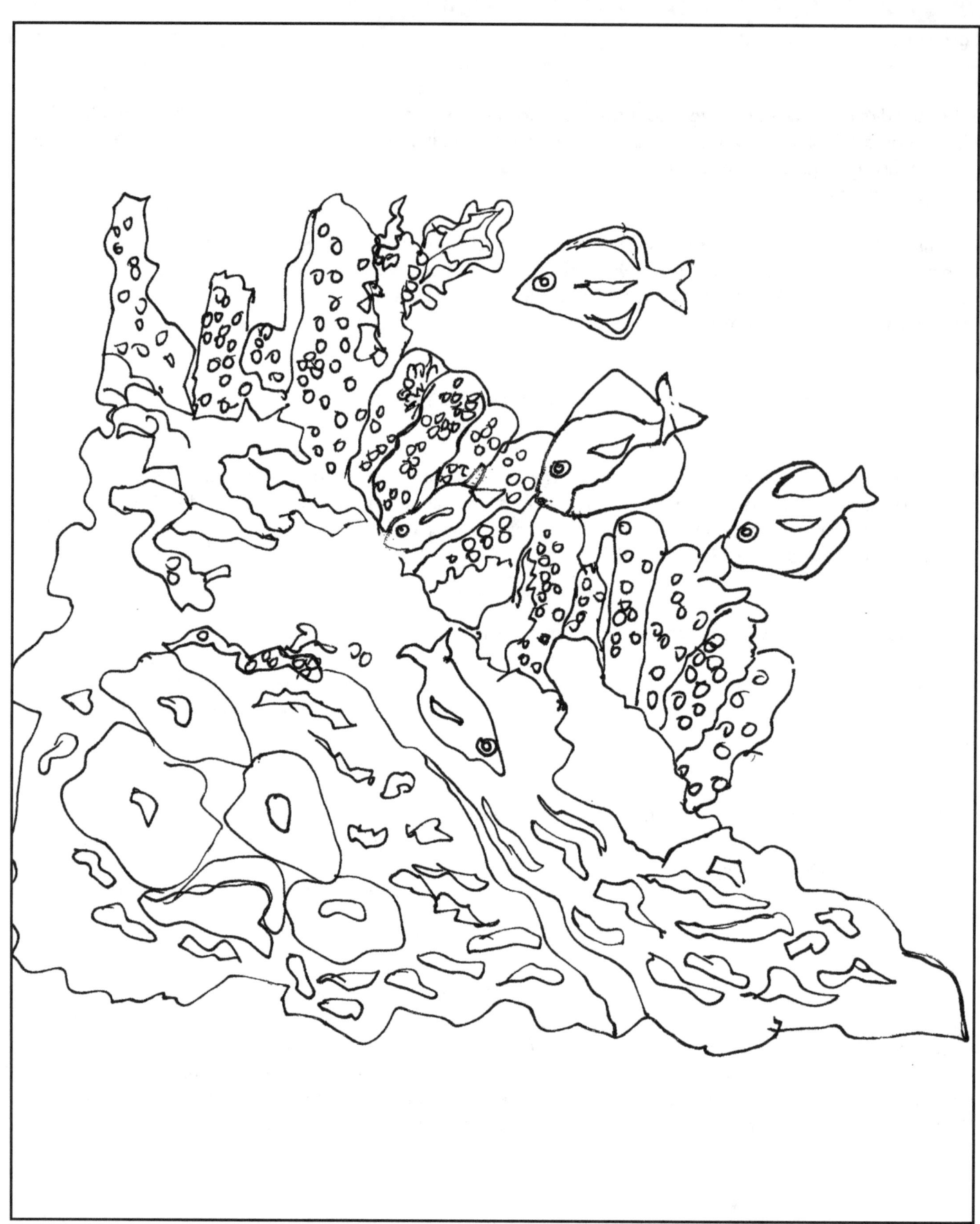

Viaport Rotterdam took over the Rotterdam Mall and has created an underwater wonderland of fish. Along with an entertainment center, the aquarium boasts many different kinds of fish in a 25,000 square feet including a clear walk through tunnel.

OLD DORP

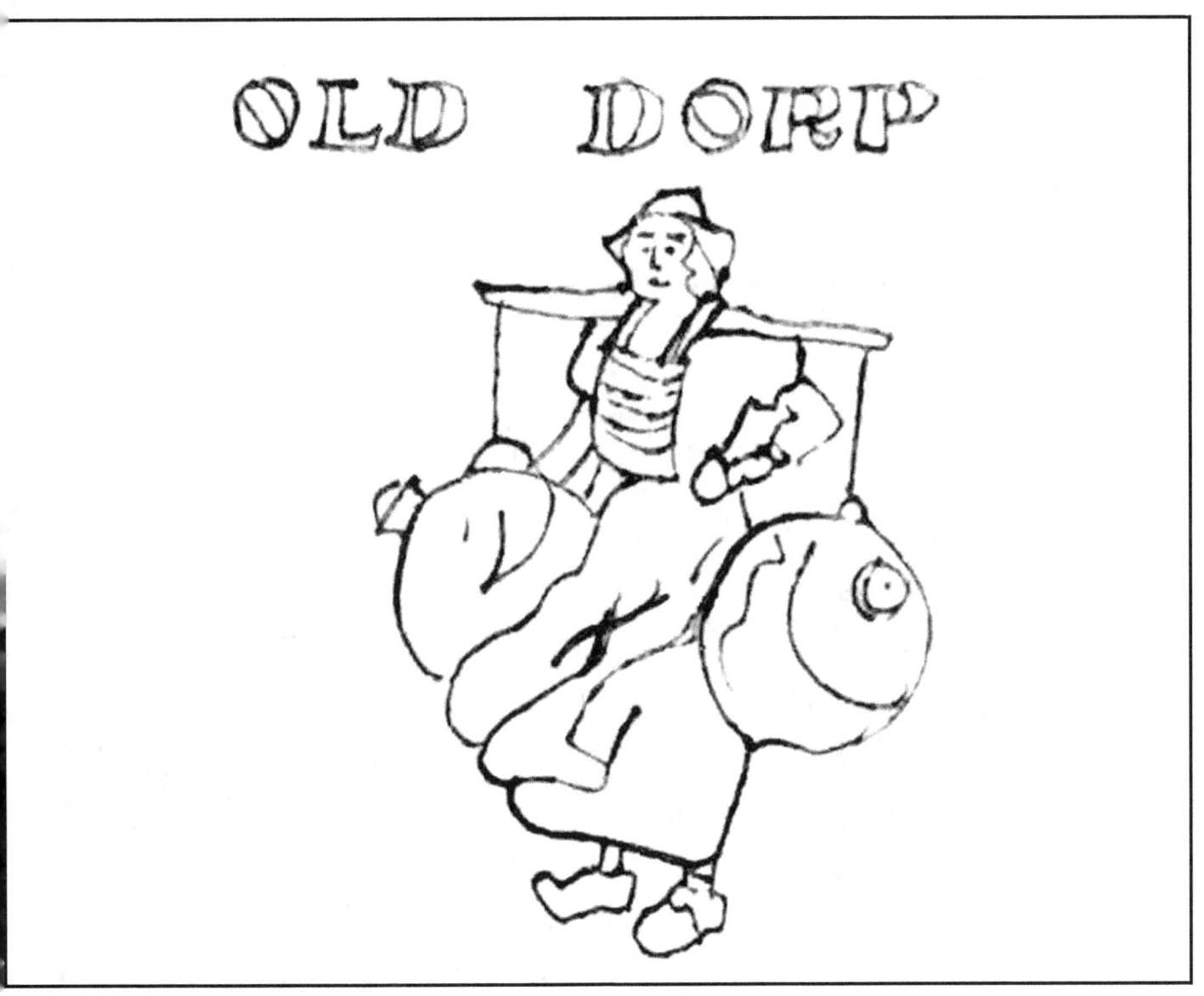

Whether you're strolling through the Stockade Historic District, Downtown State St., Union College or Central Park, taking in a world class show at Proctors, pub crawling around Erie Blvd., admiring the stunning architecture of an old house on Union St, or dining at a 100 year old restaurant or a brand new one, take a minute and really looks at your surroundings. Chances are there's a bit of history and old world charm right in front of you. There are new things happening in Schenectady too. A residential/retail/entertainment complex is being built on what is now called Mohawk Harbor. An aquarium is being installed in the old Rotterdam Mall. It's slowly becoming a destination again.

We also are blessed with world class artists here. I'm always amazed at the level of talent here; be it on canvas, paper, film or sculpture. New art venues are coming in (Breathinglights.com) and more are on the horizon. I myself am a watercolorist and a silk painter…maryfrancesmillet.com.

It is an honor to help keep the history of Old Dorp (Dutch for "town") alive for generations to come not just through reading but through the relaxing act of coloring. I could not possibly include every business or place of interest so I'm certain there will be a sequel!

If you would like to be featured in the next one or have a story to share, please let me know.

Mary Frances Millet maryfrancesmillet511@gmail.com

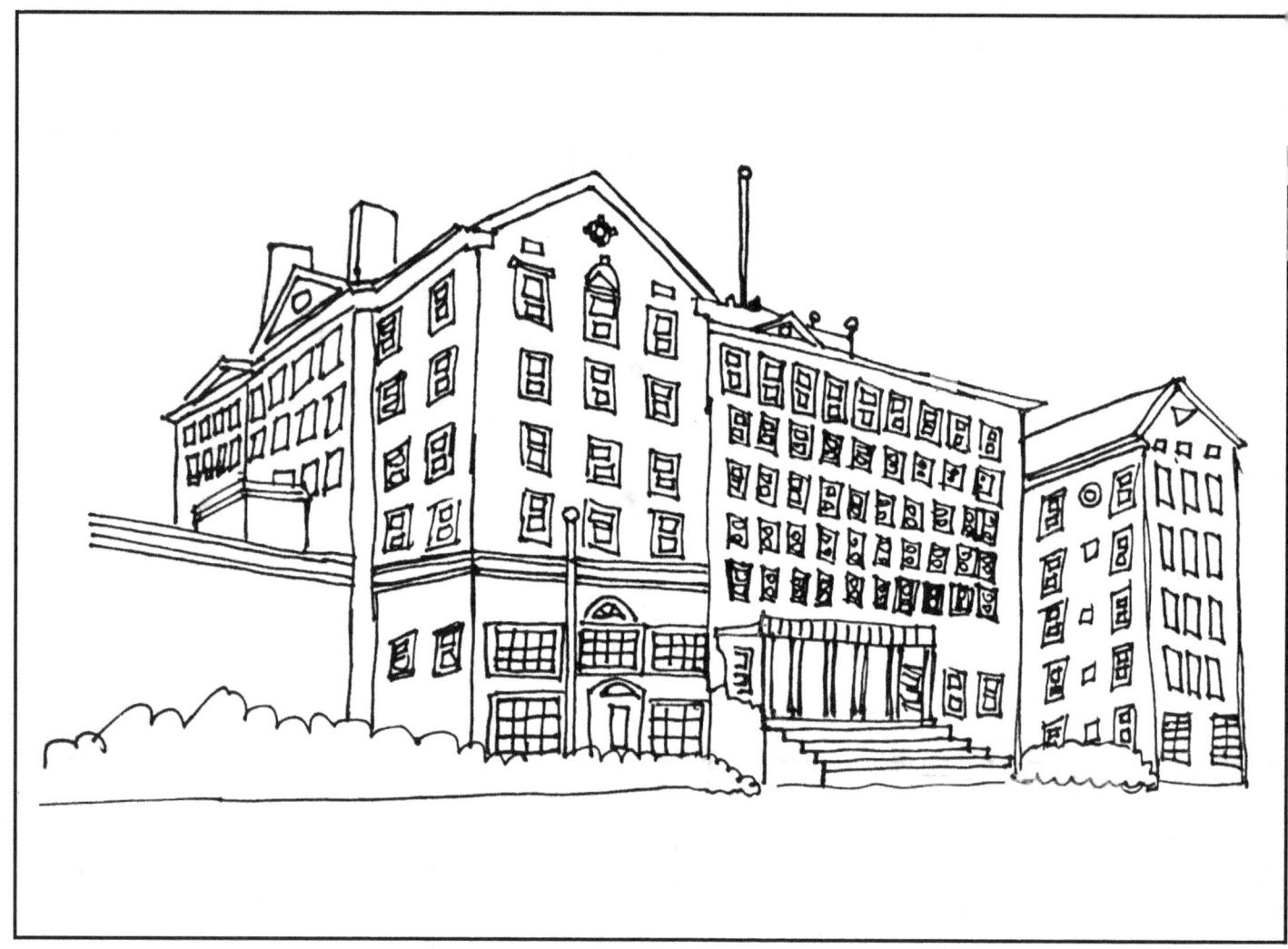

92 years old, The Hotel Van Curler is a massive brick building now occupied by Schenectady Community College. It was a popular lunch spot for General Electric employees, extravagant parties or weddings, and a place to stay overnight for notable guests including Franklin D. Roosevelt and Robert F. Kennedy.

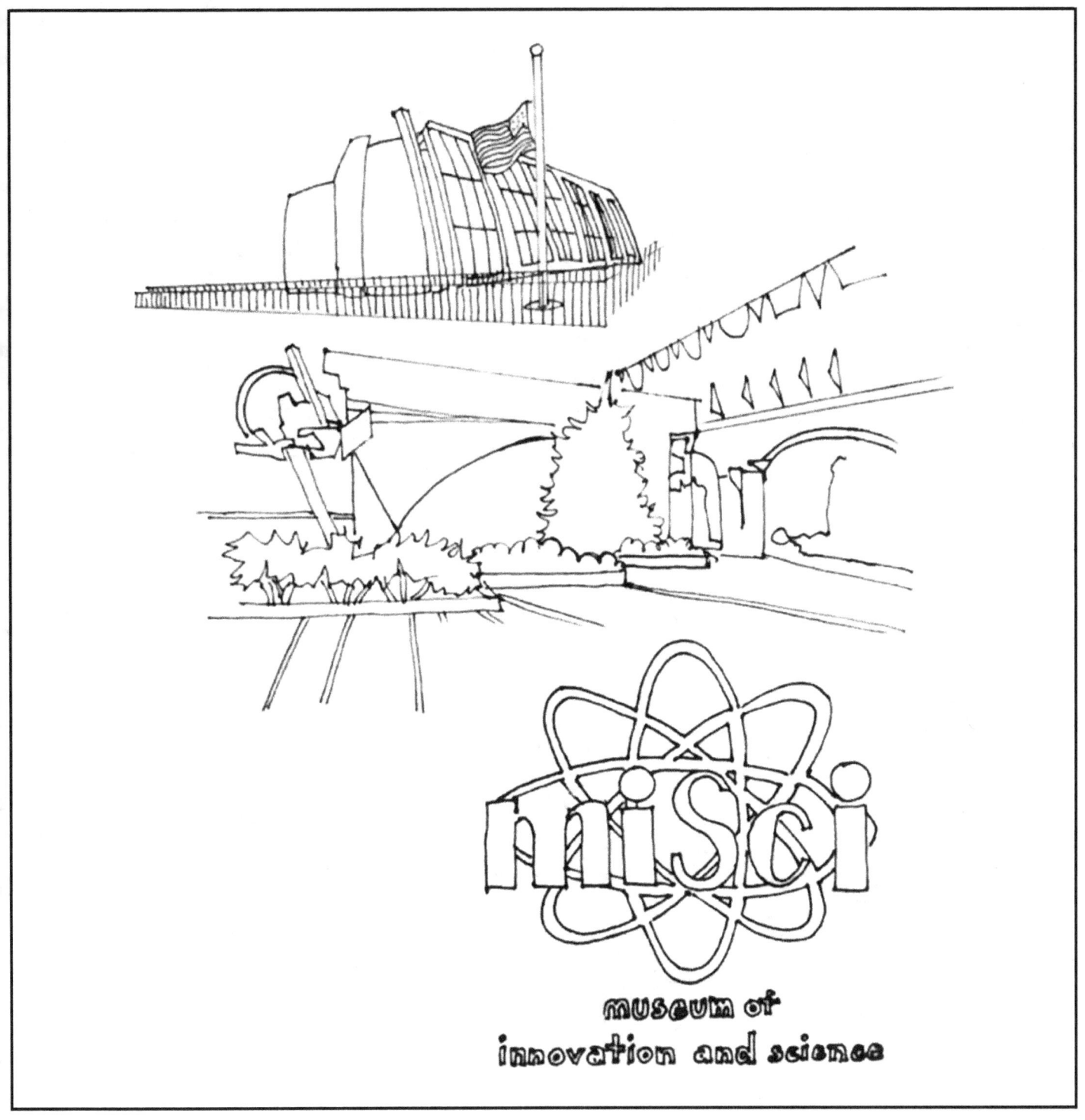

The Schenectady County Library, established 1894, became a county library in 1949. Originally the library was designed by Werner Feibes. Recently a modern Children's Wing was designed and added by the Schenectady firm Re4orm Architecture. In addition to books, magazines, movies, computer use and much more, the library also has newspapers in paper and microfilm dating back to the 1800s. You can also perform genealogy research as well.

MiSci is another Schenectady institution that houses our town's history. With a planetarium and ongoing exhibits, MiSci is a must-see. But it is much more, it is our time capsule for science and technology that this town has contributed to the world. The International Technology Archives at miSci includes more than 15,000 patents, millions of advertising documents and business records, 1,000 motion picture films, and 5,000 books, in addition to its internationally-known photograph collection of 1.5 million photographs.

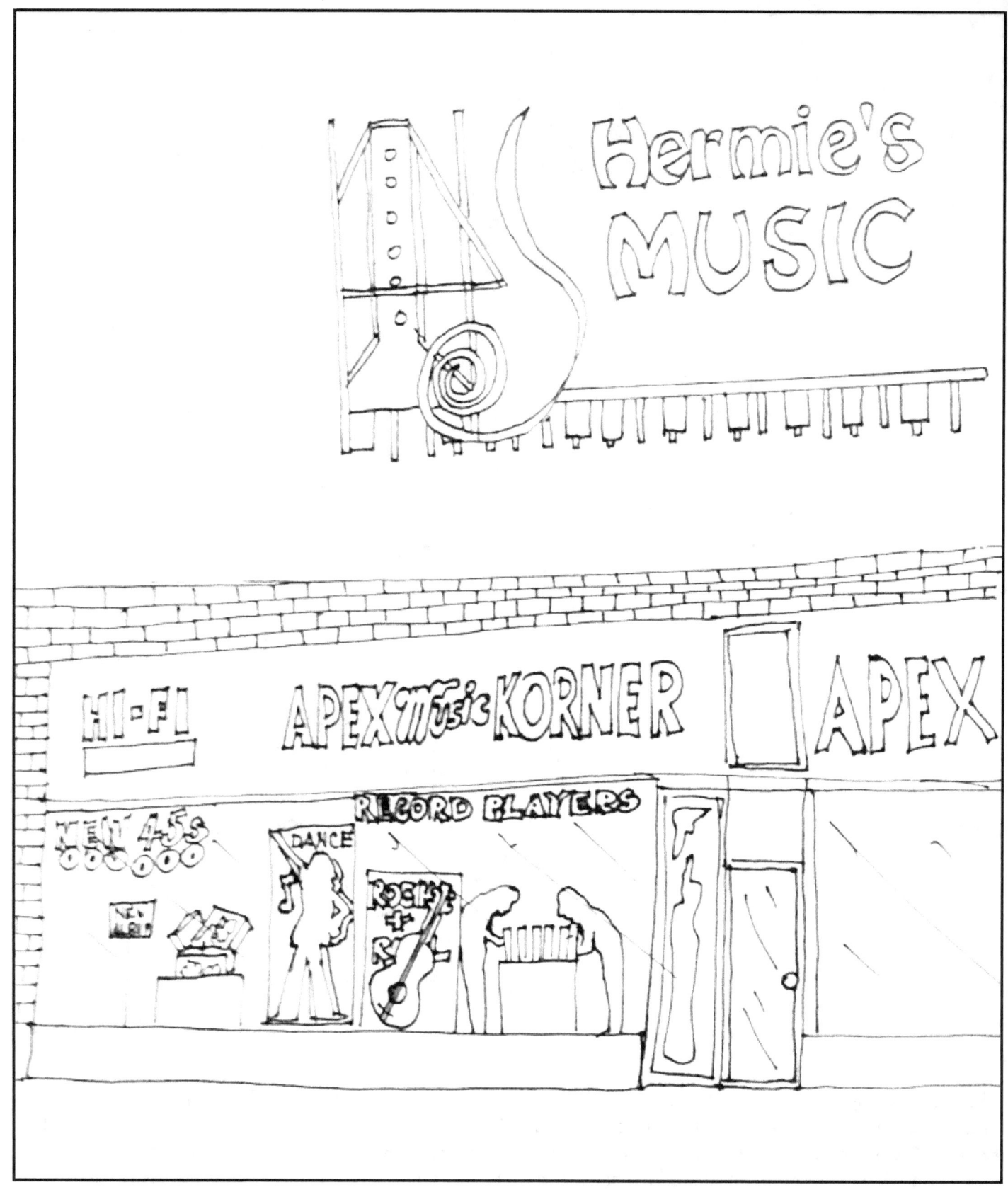

Hermies Music Store, originally on State St for decades, is still rockin after 65 years in business, but now on Jay St teaching, renting and repairing instruments.

Apex Music Korner was a staple of the downtown scene in the 50s and 60s. Selling record players, "hi-fis", albums and 45s, it was THE place to get your favorite song.

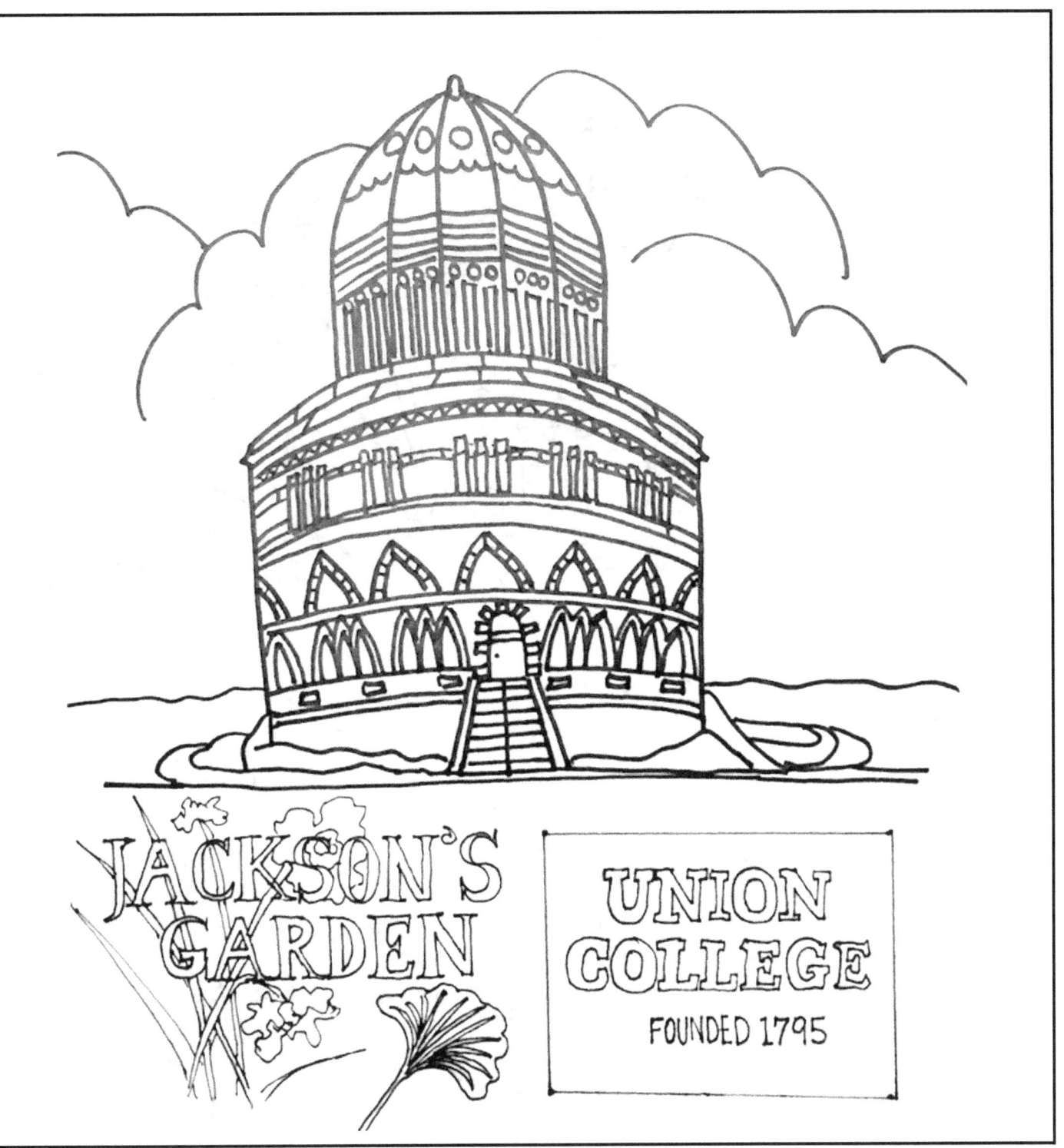

Union College, first founded in 1795, was the first institution of higher learning chartered by the New York State Board of Regents. and the first non-denominational college in the U.S. The Nott Memorial, built in 1858, is an outstanding example of Victorian architecture. It is a 16 sided brick building, with windows all around. It was conceived by President Eliphalet Nott in consultation with the French architect Joseph Ramée, who created the master plan for Union's campus. It is eighty-nine feet in diameter and capped with a ribbed dome. The dome has 709 small colored glass windows, or "illuminators." Girding the lower portion of the dome is a band of red slates bearing a modified inscription from the Talmud. In its simplest translation, the phrase says, "the day is short, the work is great, the reward is much, the Master is urgent."

Jacksons Garden was founded by Isaac Jackson in 1831 and is tended by a full time gardener. It is home to an 80 ft. ancient ginkgo tree and is the only planned garden on a college campus in the US.

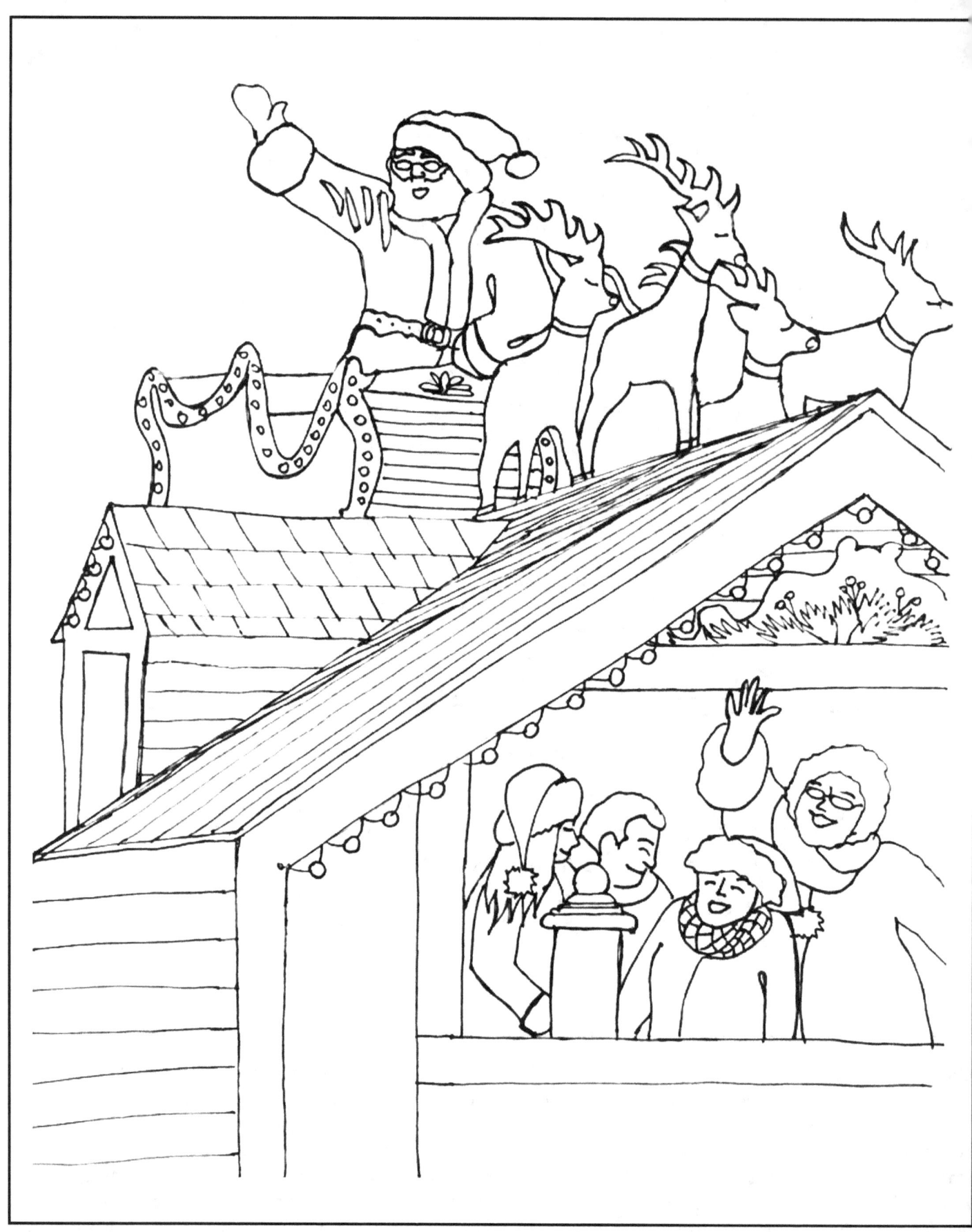

Schenectady's Christmas Parade is the biggest night time holiday parade in the Northeast. Now in its 49th year, it starts at SCCC and progresses up State St. Held for 2 hours, rain or shine, it includes more than 100 floats, bands, marchers, dance troupes, and decorated vehicles vying for seven top prizes.

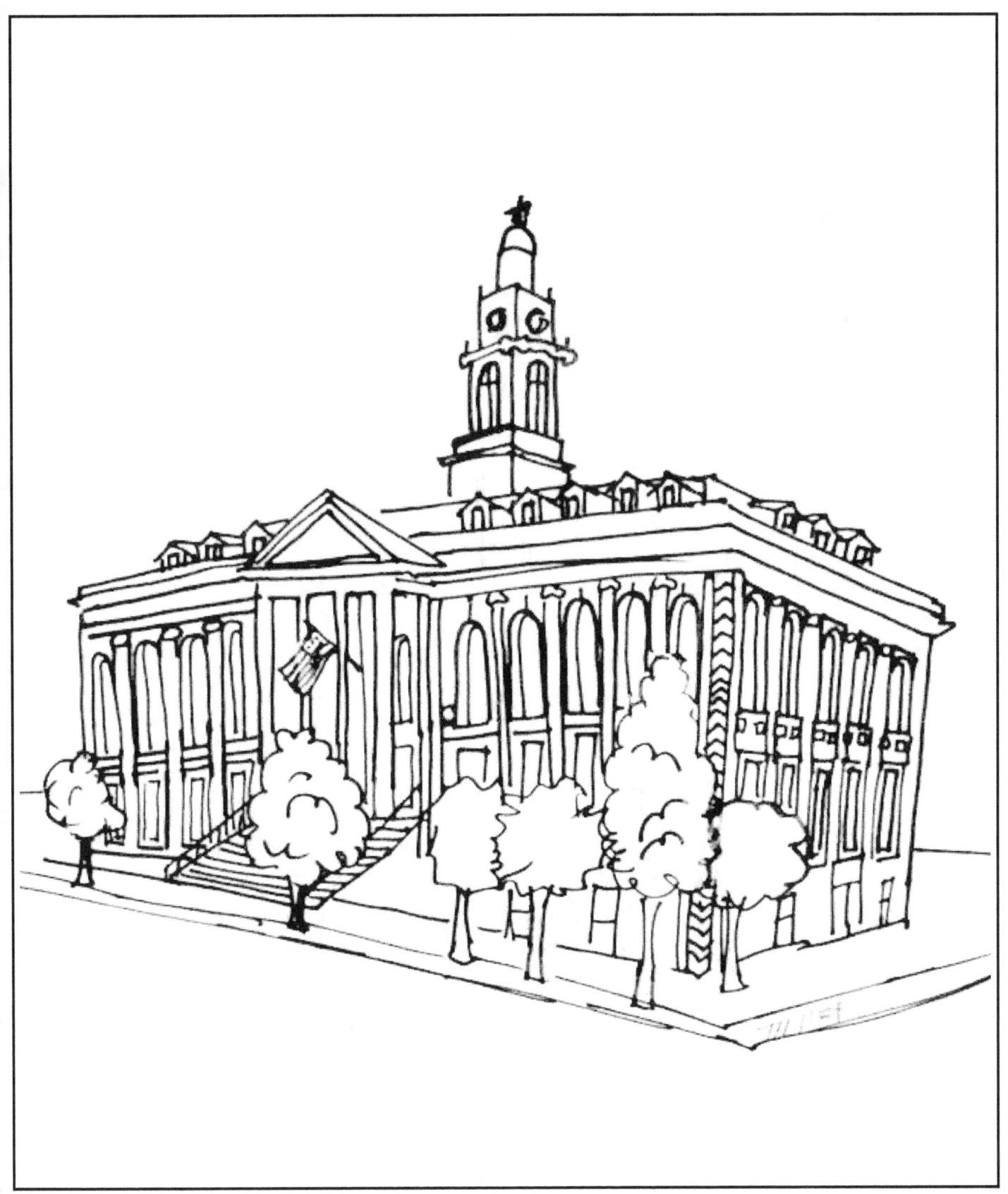

Schenectady City Hall is the seat of government of the city of Schenectady. Designed by McKim, Mead, and White, the building was constructed around 1932. It is a gorgeous piece of architecture, inside and out, built in a revival of the Federal Style. Its most prominent features include the square clock tower, with its gold-leaf dome and weathervane, and the Ionic neoclassical portico. It was listed on the National Register of Historic Places in 1978.

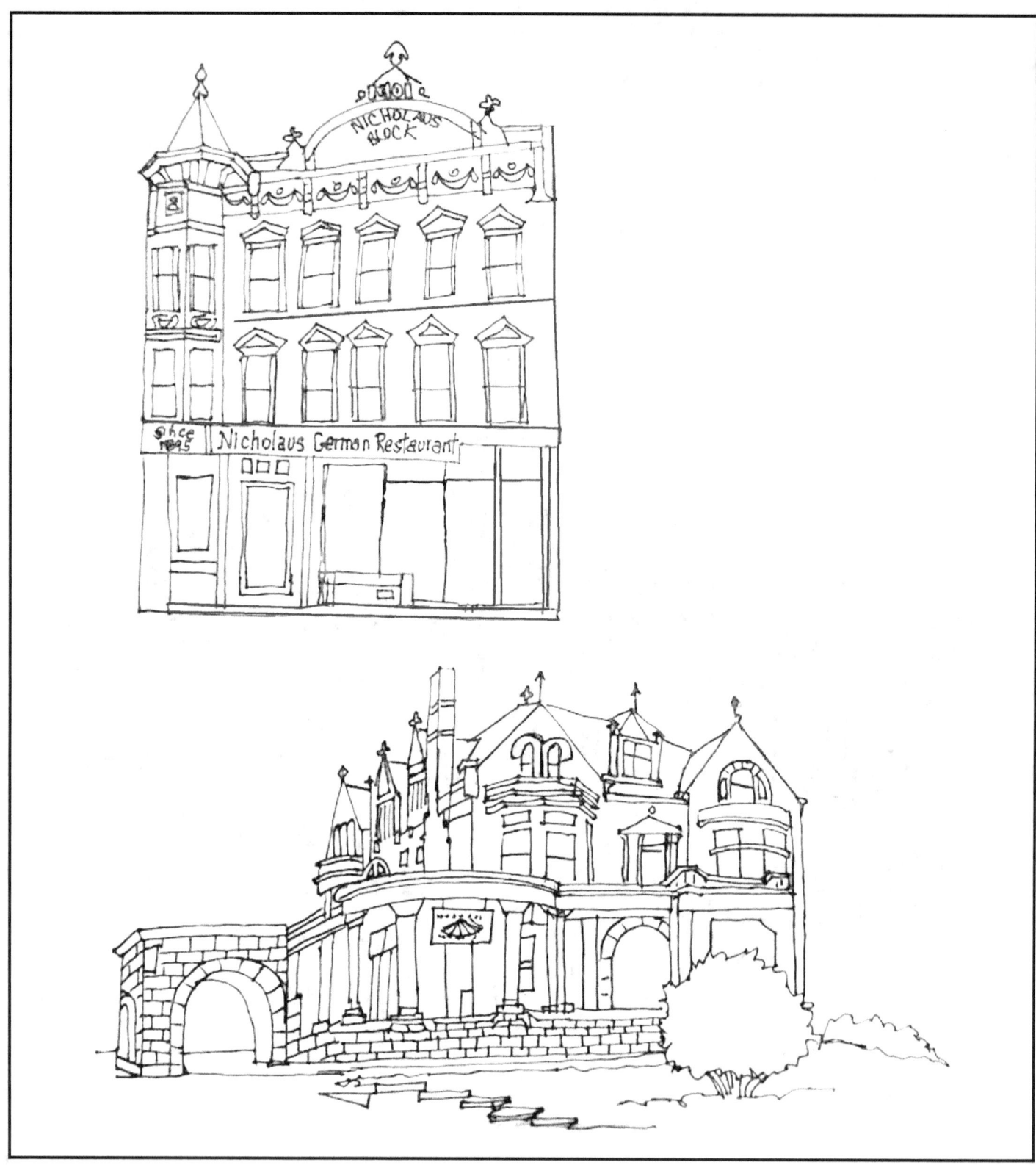

Nicholaus German Restaurant was first opened as a saloon by Louis Nicholaus in the 1800s. It was moved from Liberty and Ferry Streets to its current location on Erie Blvd until it closed in 1975. In the early days, only men were served at the elegant mahogany bar. Women were allowed in later. Built in 1955, the Veterans of World Wars building at 718 Union St. is a beautiful example of red brick and architectural embellishments.

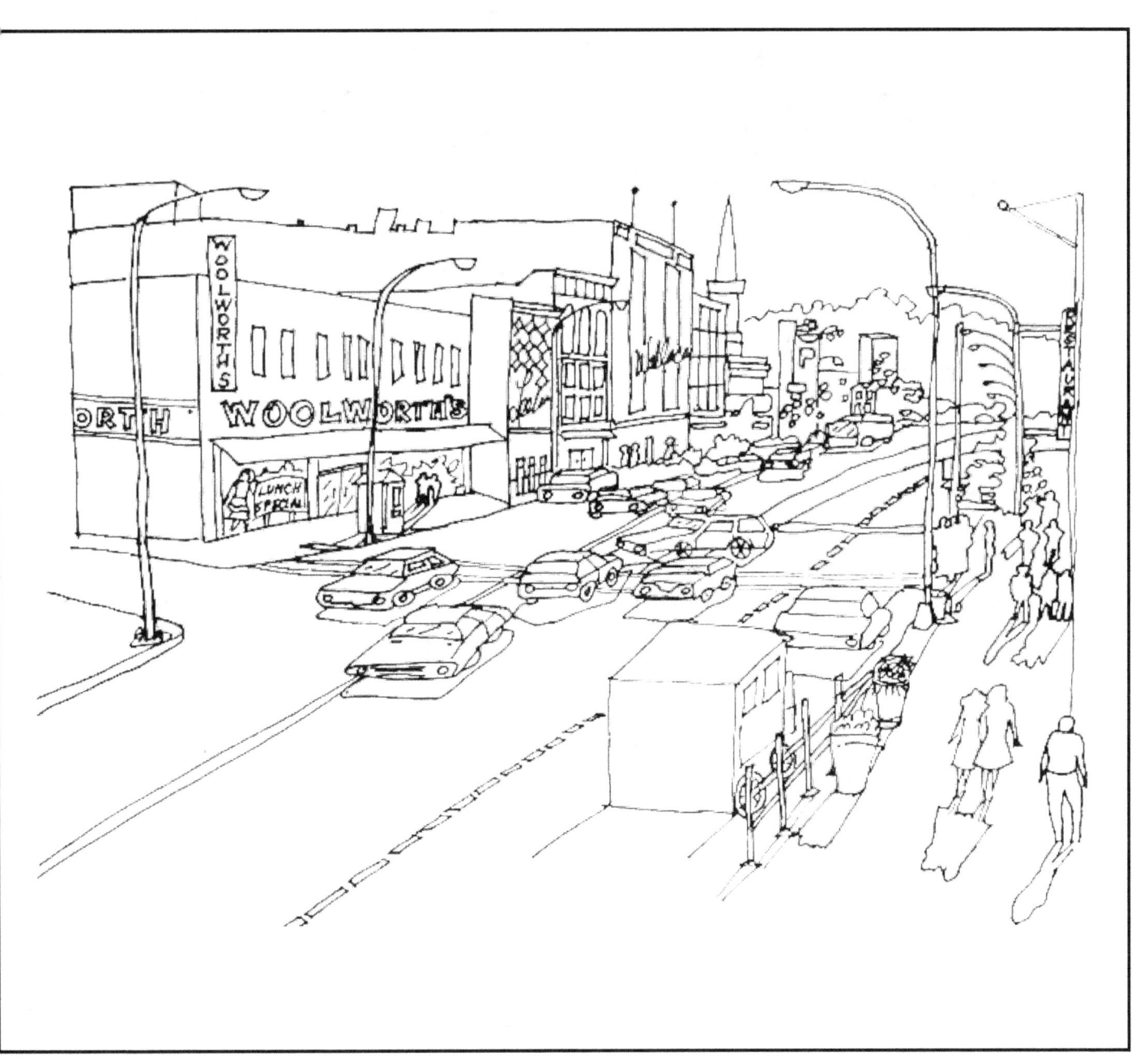

Downtown Schenectady State St. streetscape circa 1975.

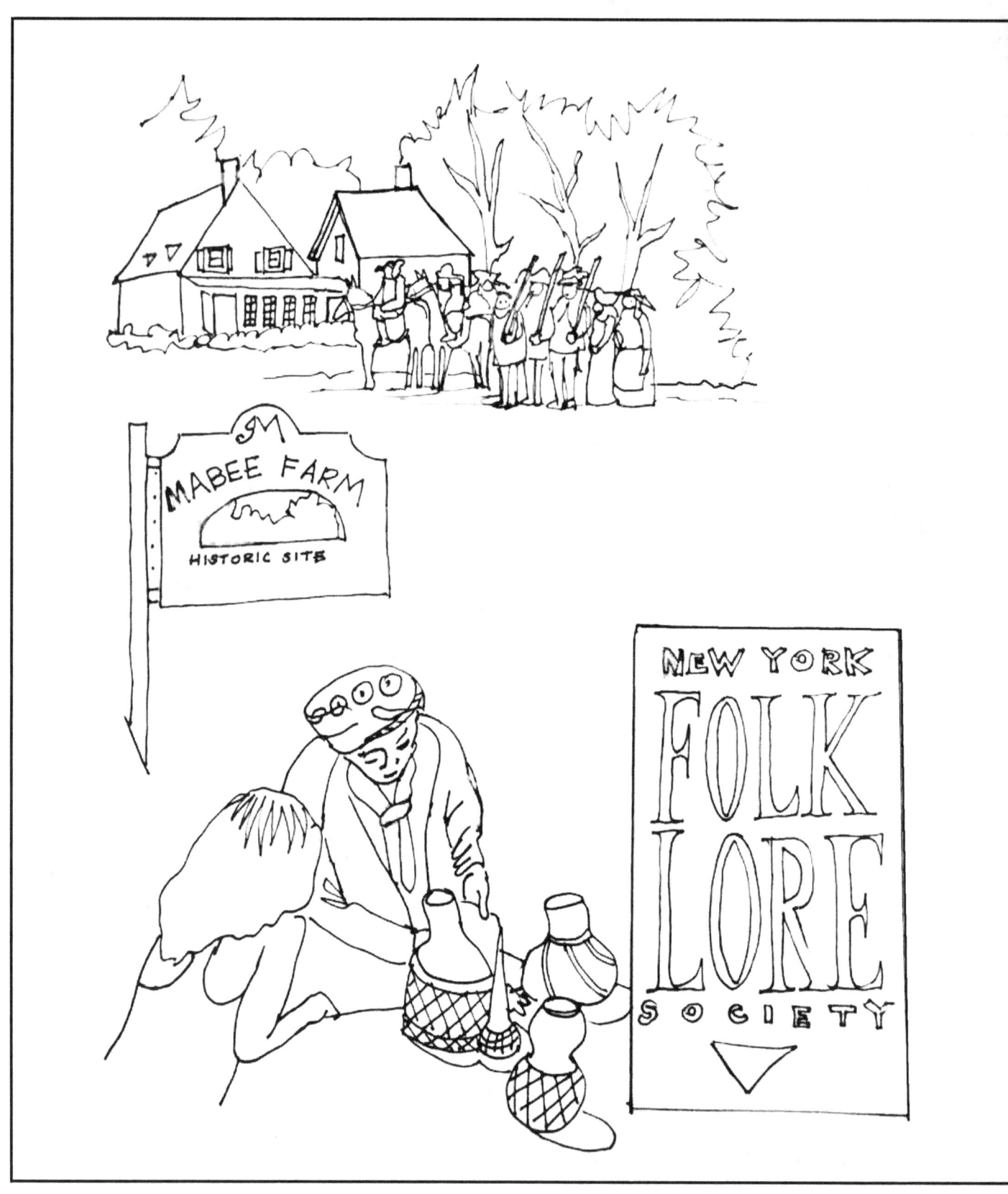

Experience what life was like in the 1700s here in Schenectady County at the historic Mabee Farm Reenactments of the Revolutionary War battles have volunteers in period dress turning the site into a military encampment with colonial militia, British Loyalists, Native Americans and local settlers.

The Folklore Society on Jay St, opened in 1944 and relocated to Schenectady in 1999. It is the state's authority on NY's diverse cultures and its' folklorists, folk artists, folk arts enthusiasts, and people working in other areas of the arts and culture.

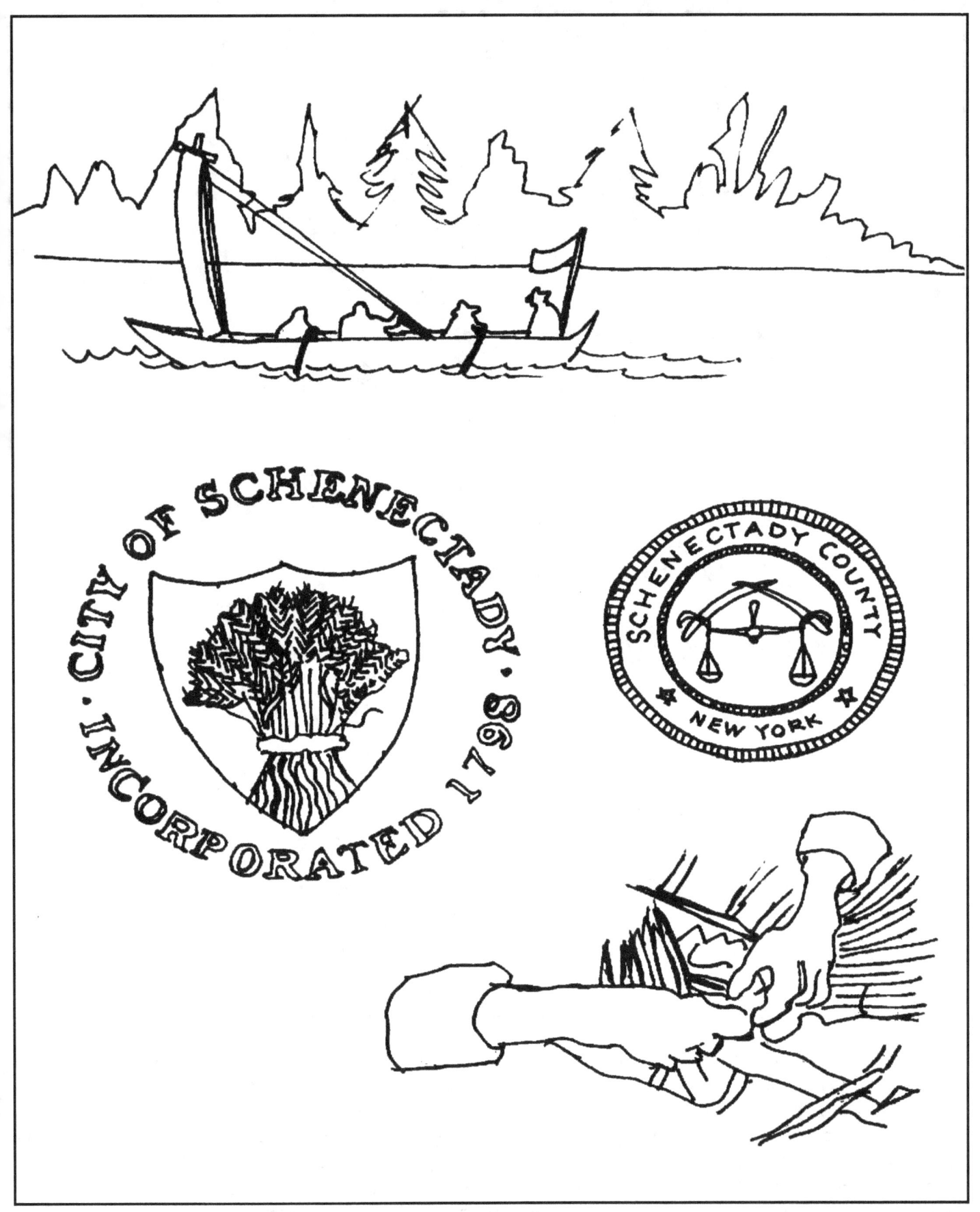

Clockwise from top: the "Schenectady" boat on the Mohawk River, a smaller, lighter version of the Durham boat made for transporting goods in shallow waters; city flag; craftsperson in the early days of the broom making industry, city seal depicting a shaft of straw for making brooms.

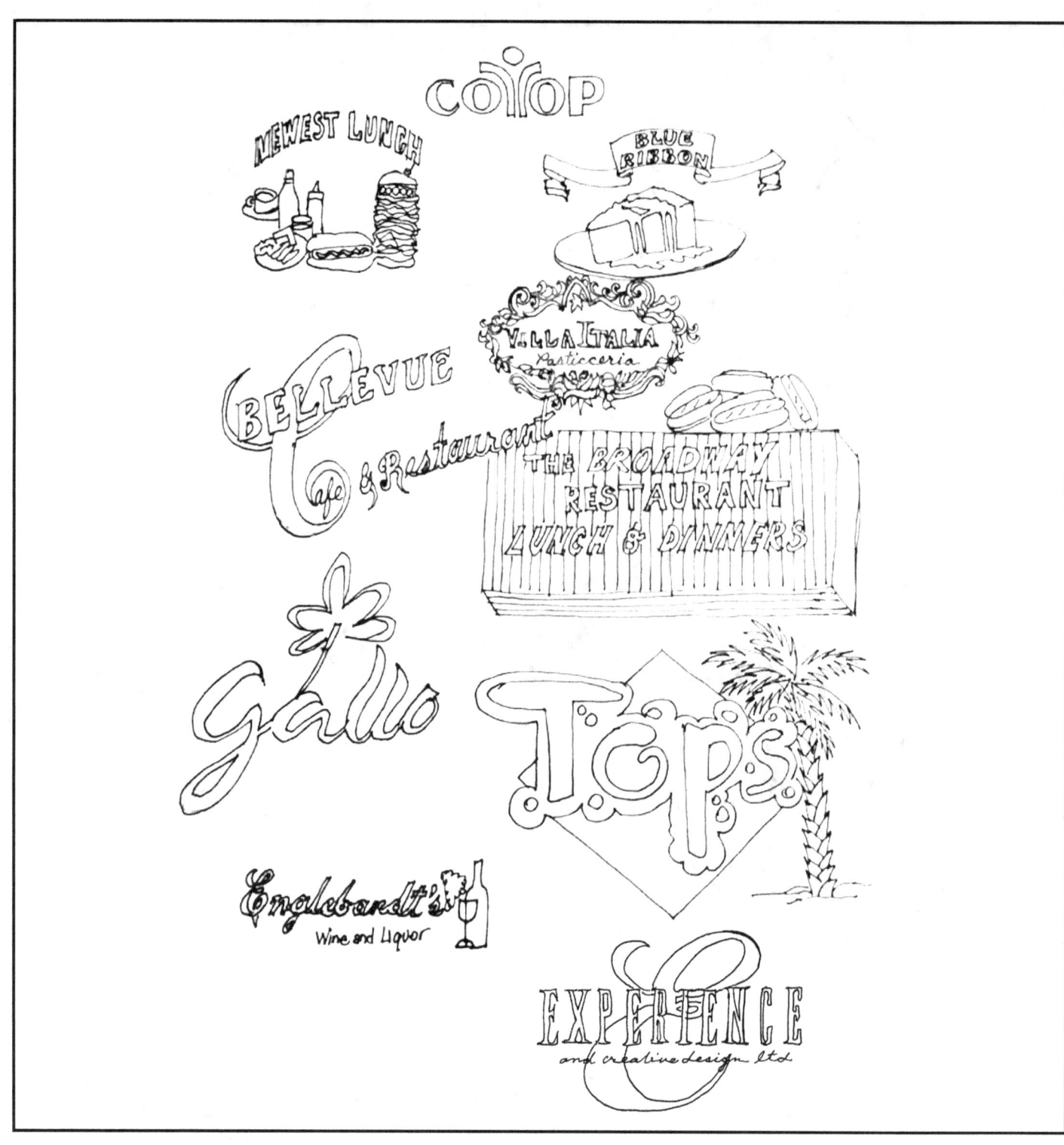

Blue Ribbon Diner, opened in 1977, is home of one of the best cheesecakes in town. Villa italia, owned by the Mallozzi family, is home to gelato, coffee and an amazing assortment of the most decadent pastries (as well as the Emmy from Ray Romano's "Everybody Loves Raymond." Gallo and Son Florist has been delivering flowers in Schenectady since 1930. Newest Lunch: Famous for hotdogs since 1921. The Coop Market has been loyally serving our community with a wide variety of foods and baked goods since 1943. Broadway Lunch, a wonderfully old diner on (where else?) Broadway has its own hearty brand of hotdogs and meat sauce. (I see a pattern here…) A nicely decorated diner with palm trees and modern touches, Tops has been around since 1962. Bellevue Cafe has been a comfort food stop for lunch and dinner for 30+ years. Englebardt's Liquors has been open since 1946 and serves wine tastings from the cuvenee wine system. 19 year old Experience and Creative Design lures you in with its big-city style window displays. You're hooked once you walk into this enchanting world of floral design, art and decor To. Die. For.

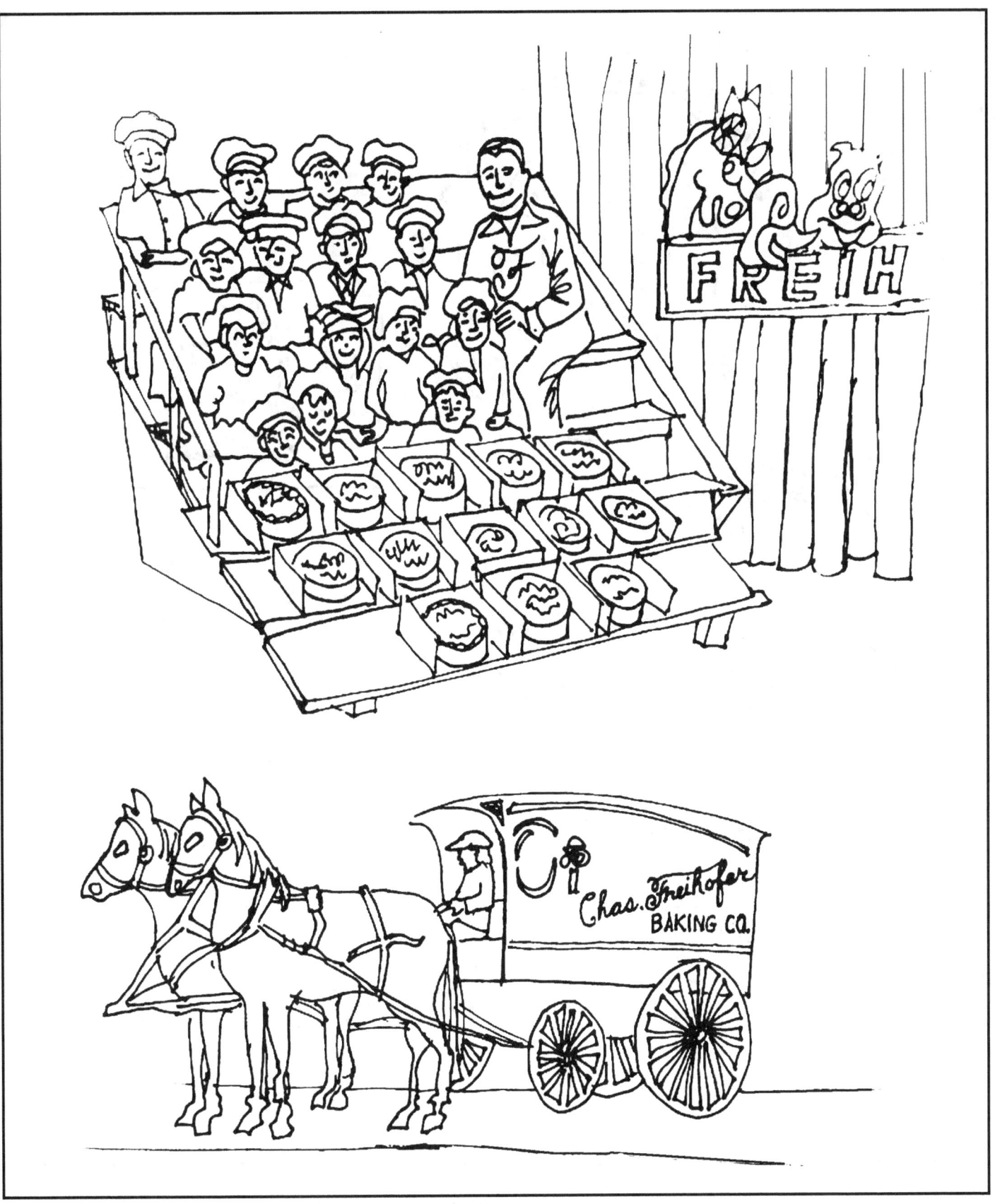

Charles Freihofer Baking Co started horse drawn delivery service in Lansingburgh in 1913. Their success can be attributed in part due to their early generosity. Soon after they opened, a flood left people stranded without food or water. The company provided free bread to the flood victims. A second location was opened in Schenectady in 1914. The "Breadtime Stories" TV show for kids on WRGB was hosted by Uncle Jim Fisk from 1949 to 1966.

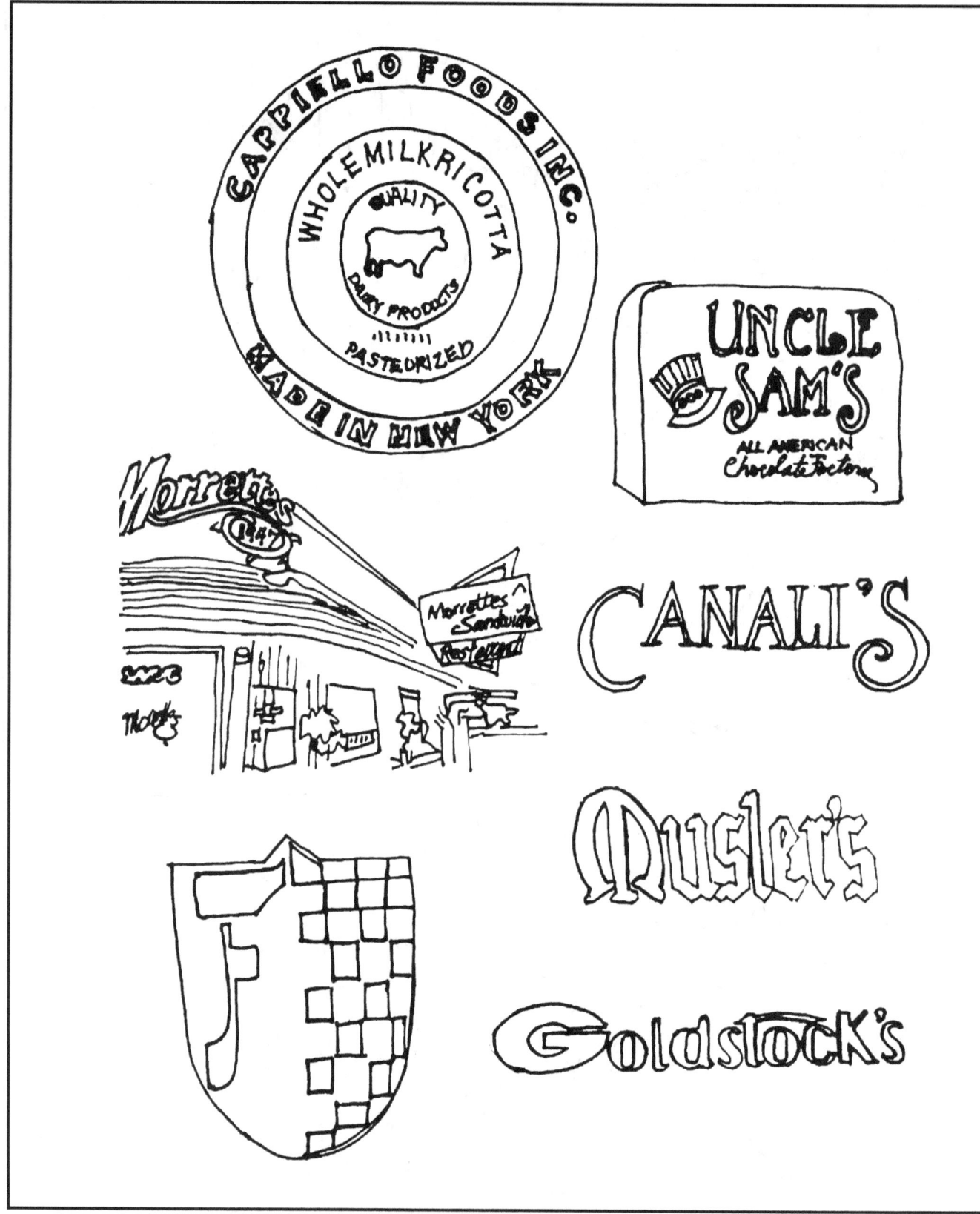

Ferarris is an iconic old Italian restaurant where large portions of the best Italian food in town is the norm. Going on 90 years, Uncle Sam's Chocolates still delights us with an assortment of handmade chocolate. Canali's has been one of our best Italian restaurants since 1946. Cappiello Foods is 100 years old! Look for the cow on top of the building on Broadway and be prepared to be overcome with the enticing aromas of fine Italian foods within. Muslers has been in business over 90 years starting on State St. near Proctors and moving to Union St. in 1991. Goldstock's Sporting Goods has been in business for over 100 years. First open on Broadway, it now resides in Scotia.

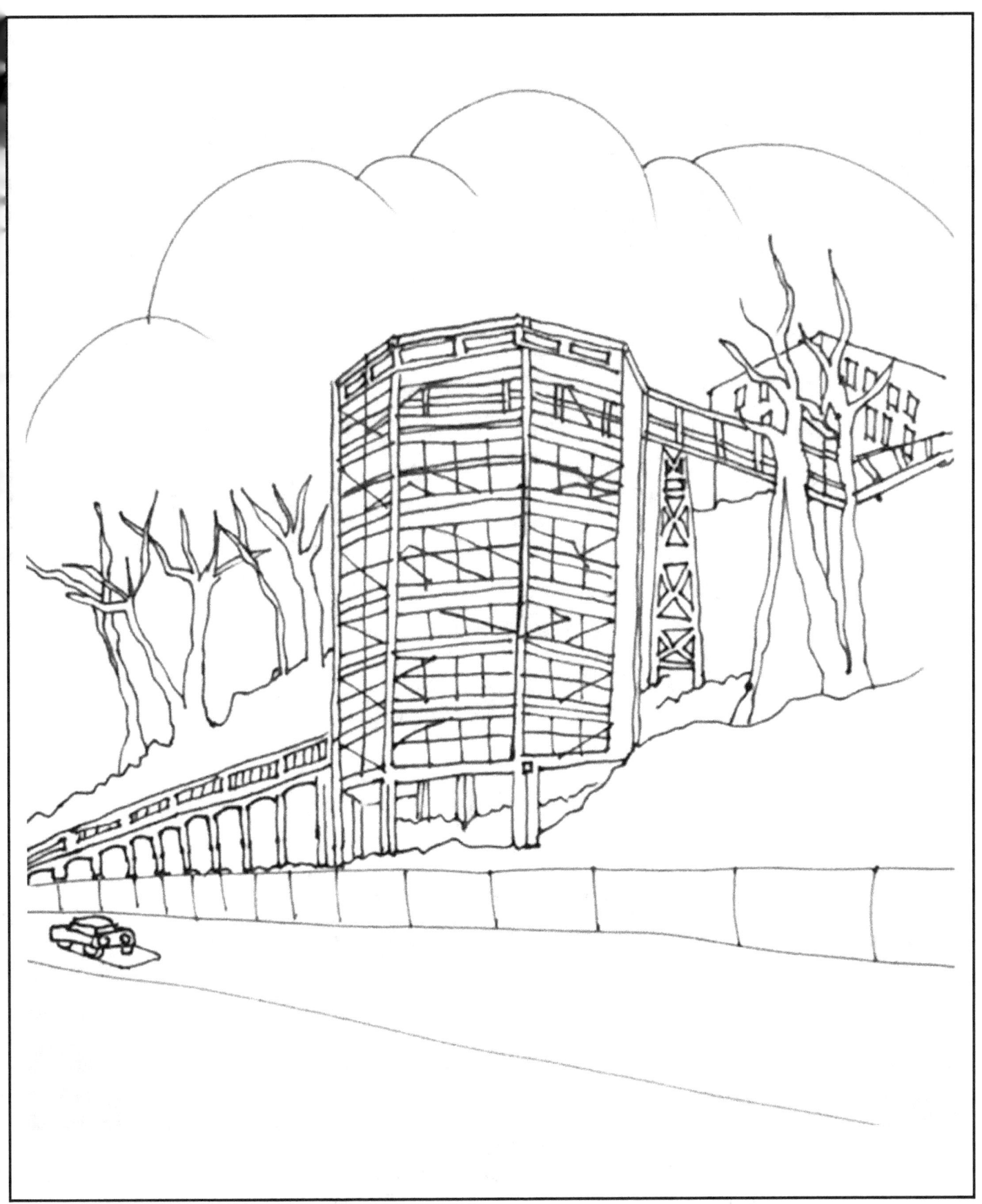

The Klondike Ramp at the corner of Broadway and 890 was constructed in the 1930s as a walkway before cars for GE workers to get from the hills of Schenectady to the plant. Part of the stone railing is still visible at Exit 5. Rumor has it, it was named "Klondike" because of the Arctic-like wind that blew through it during cold winters.

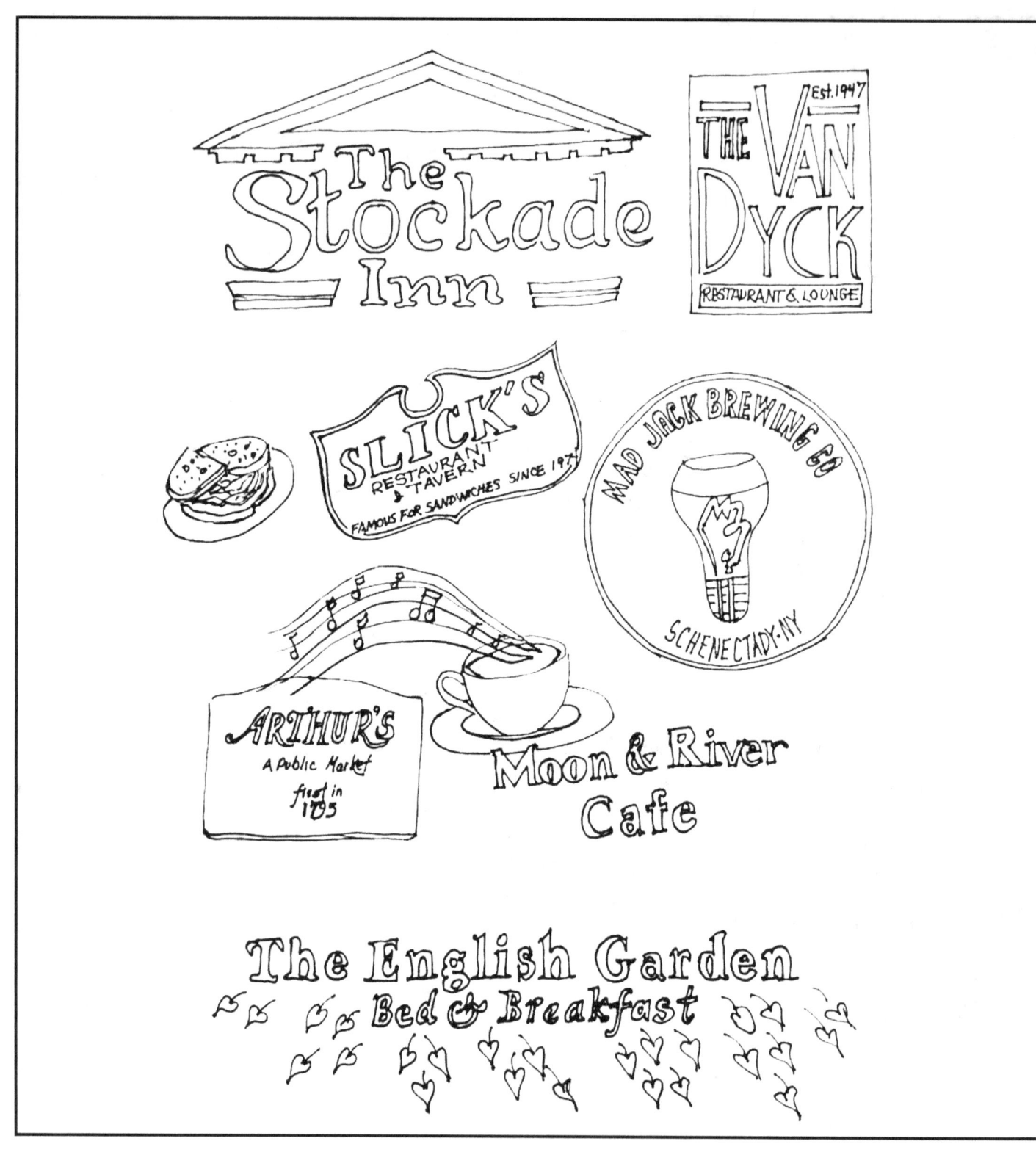

The Stockade is rich with a variety of restaurants and cafés to suit every taste. The Stockade Inn is an elegant 17th century restaurant and 18 well-appointed room boutique hotel in the Stockade. (Take a look at the polished wood angels in the lounge!) The Van Dyck is another old establishment, opened in 1947. It is considered one of the top "listening rooms" in the US. It boasts great food and live music from celebs as well as rising stars. Its' microbrewery reopened in 2011 as Mad Jack. Slicks has been around for 30 years and still astounds us with the biggest sandwiches in town. A full lb. of meat comes on each one. Come hungry. Richard Genest operates the Moon and River as well as Arthur's. Both are havens for gluten free, vegetarian, vegan and music lovers but Arthur's, opened in 1795, is considered the oldest continuously run market in the country. The English Garden Bed and Breakfast is a charming (real) period boutique hotel in the heart of the Stockade.

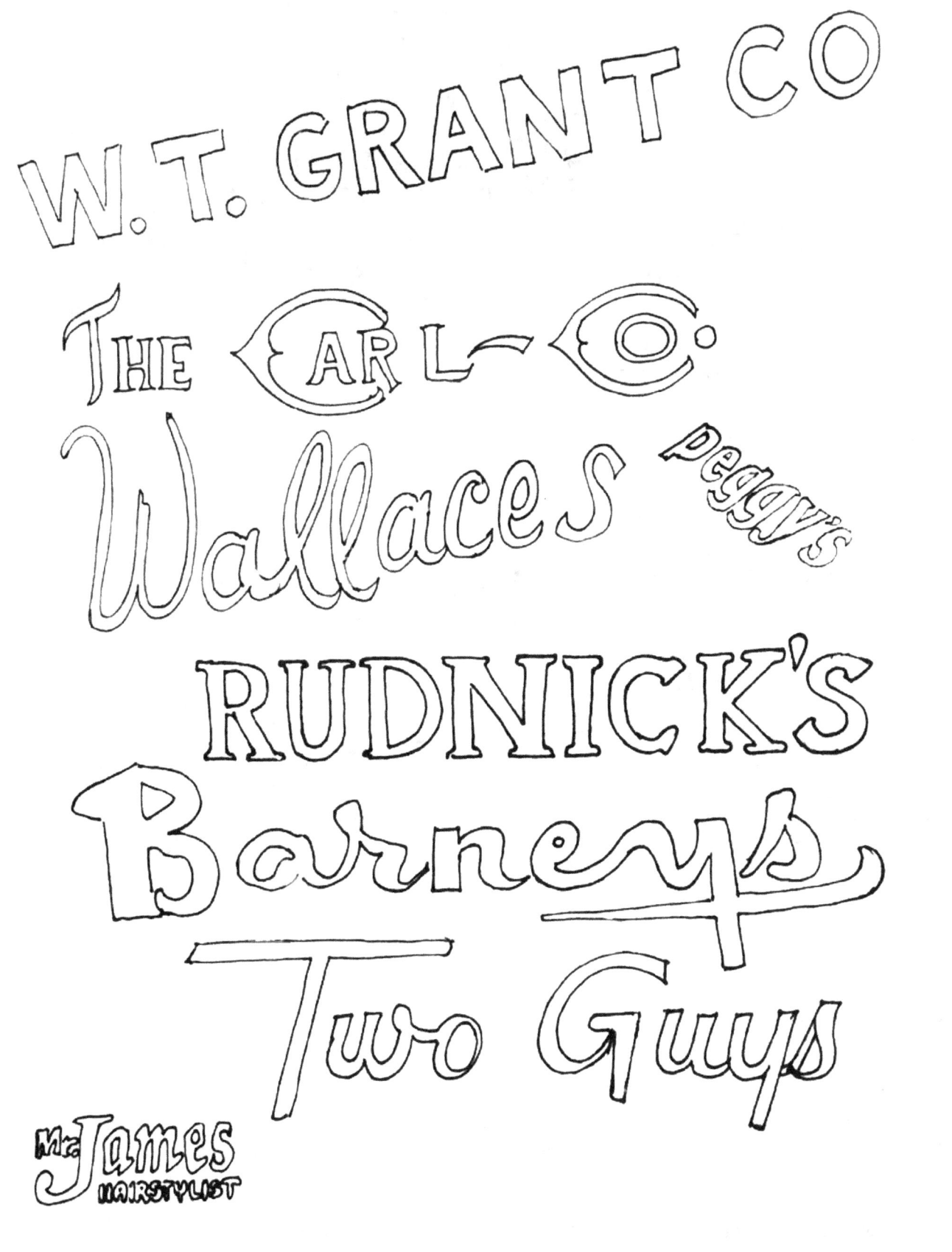

A few of the popular department stores of the era from the 50s to the 70s. (And, of course, Peggy's Restaurant) Rudnicks recently reopened after over 100 years in business.

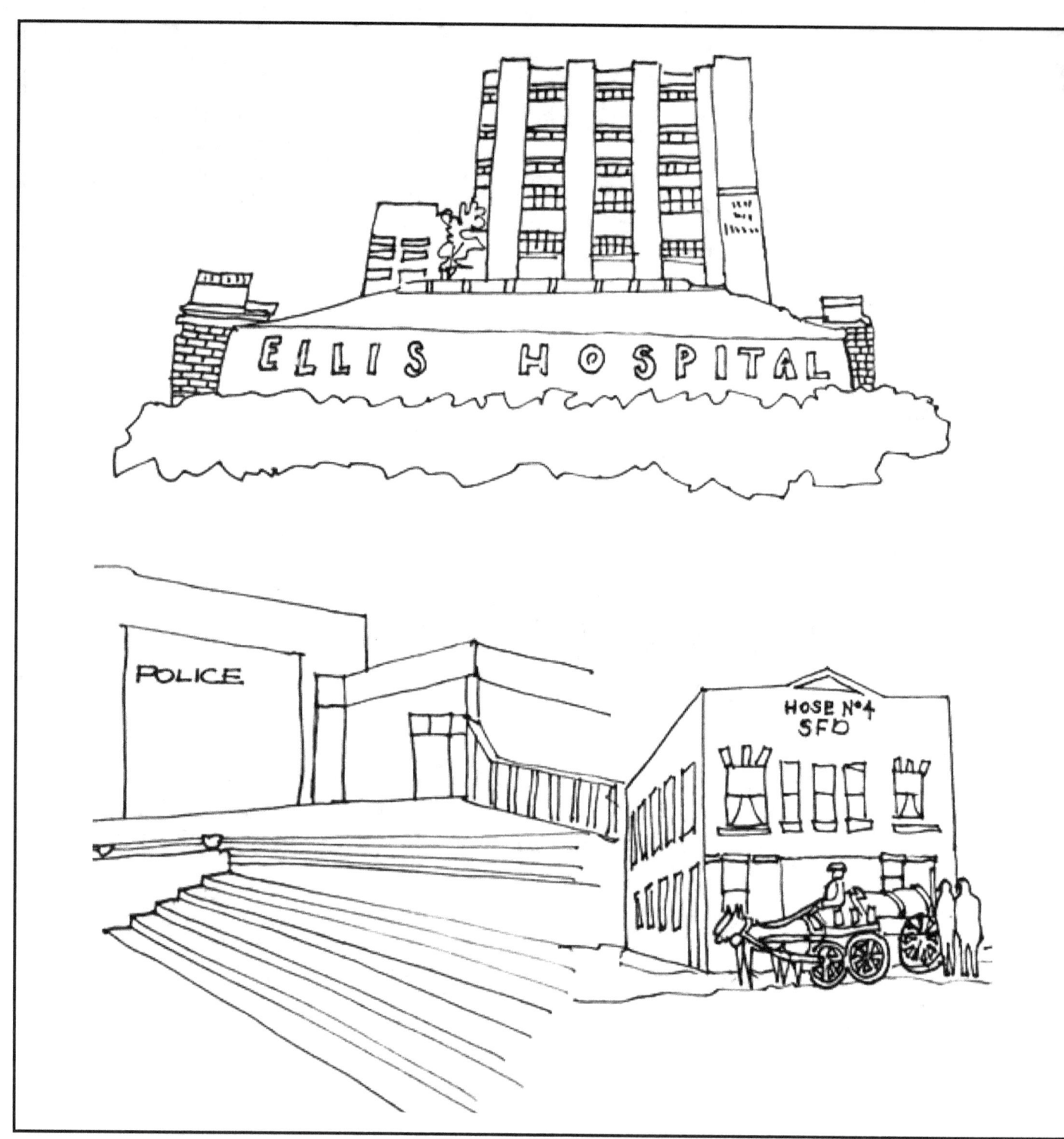

Ellis Hospital opened its doors to the community in 1885. It encompasses three main campuses and five additional service locations. Continued modernization projects include a new, state-of-the-art Emergency Department, expanded parking, a major addition to the Bellevue Woman's Center and taking over St Claire's Hospital.

The modern aesthetic of the Schenectady Police Department was designed by Werner Feibes, an architect still living in the Stockade.

Schenectady's Fire Dept covers 11 square miles. From its days of horse drawn carriage in 1900 to the modern fleet we have now, the fire department is 117 members strong.

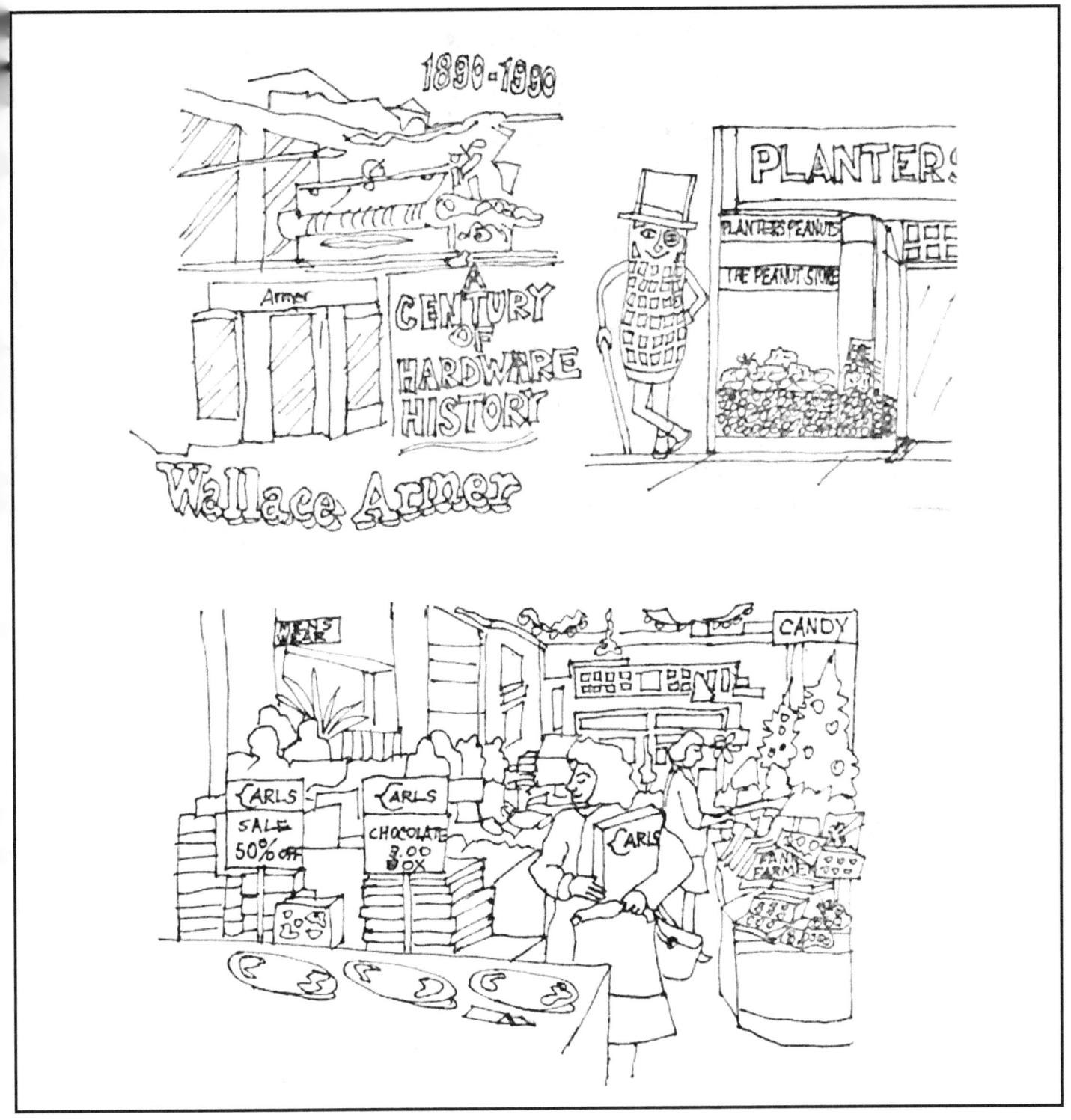

Wallace Armer Hardware Store, 1890-1990, was the go-to hardware store on Erie Blvd. It used the Landon Cash Carrier system before cash registers that consisted of a metal track that ran along the ceiling. Money was placed in the box and sent upstairs for change and a receipt.

Planters Peanuts drew shoppers in from State St with its enticing aroma of roasted nuts.

Carl Co 1906-1991, warrants a special mention due to its long standing presence in Downtown Schenectady. From its modest beginnings as a dry goods store in Medina, NY in 1891, Carl expanded to Schenectady in 1906. Carl's was the place to shop, outlasting all the other department stores on State St. Their creative Christmas window delighted shoppers for decades.

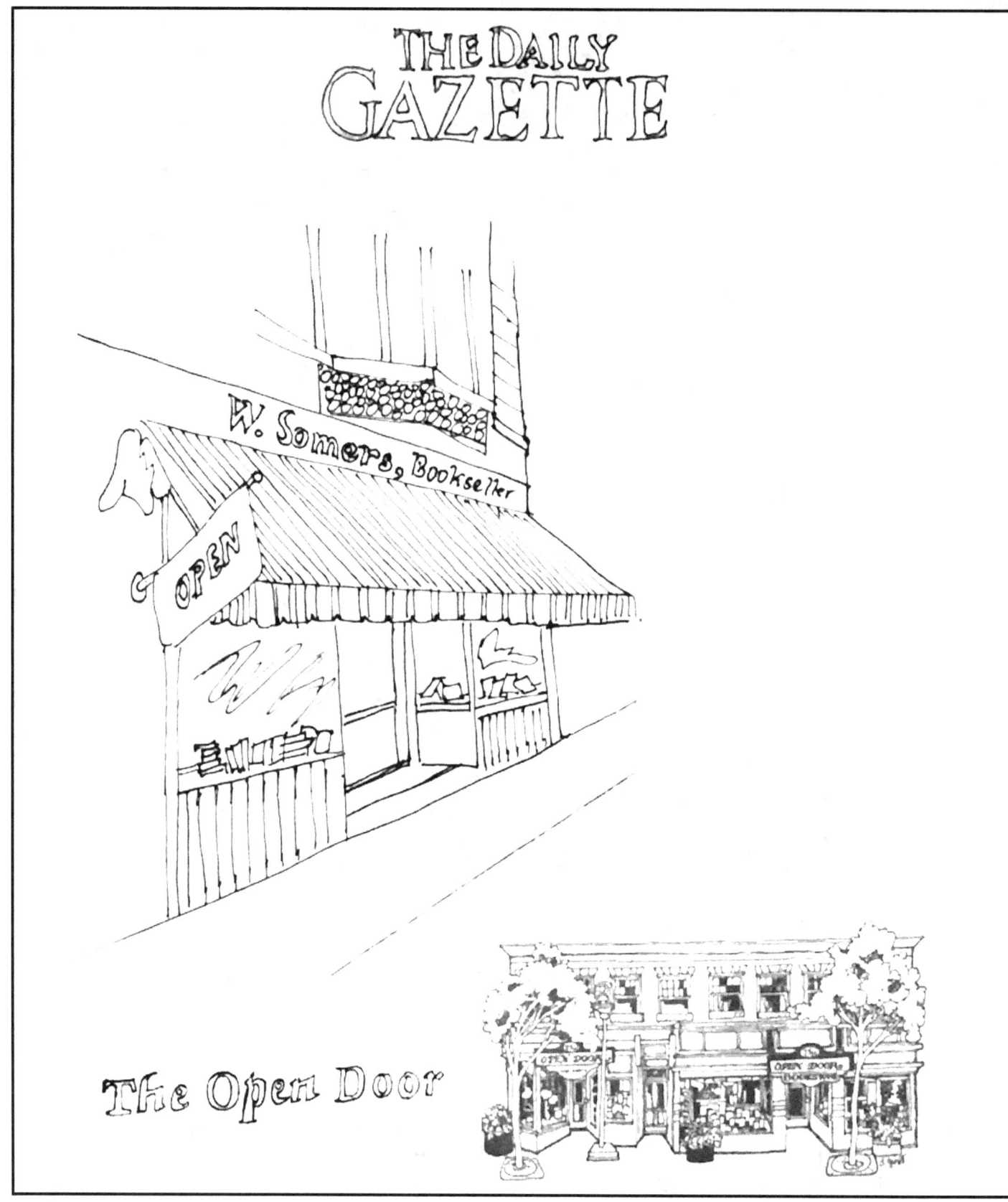

THE DAILY GAZETTE

W. Somers, Bookseller

OPEN

The Open Door

The Schenectady Gazette has been the source for news since 1894 when the Schenectady Printing Association took over a weekly called the Schenectady Gazette and turned it into a daily.

Somers Booksellers opened in 1971 and continues to have an extensive collection of books and reading materials. Wayne Somers is a fountain of knowledge about many subjects.

The Open Door is destination shopping for unusual gifts as well as books. It has been a fixture on Jay St for 45 years.

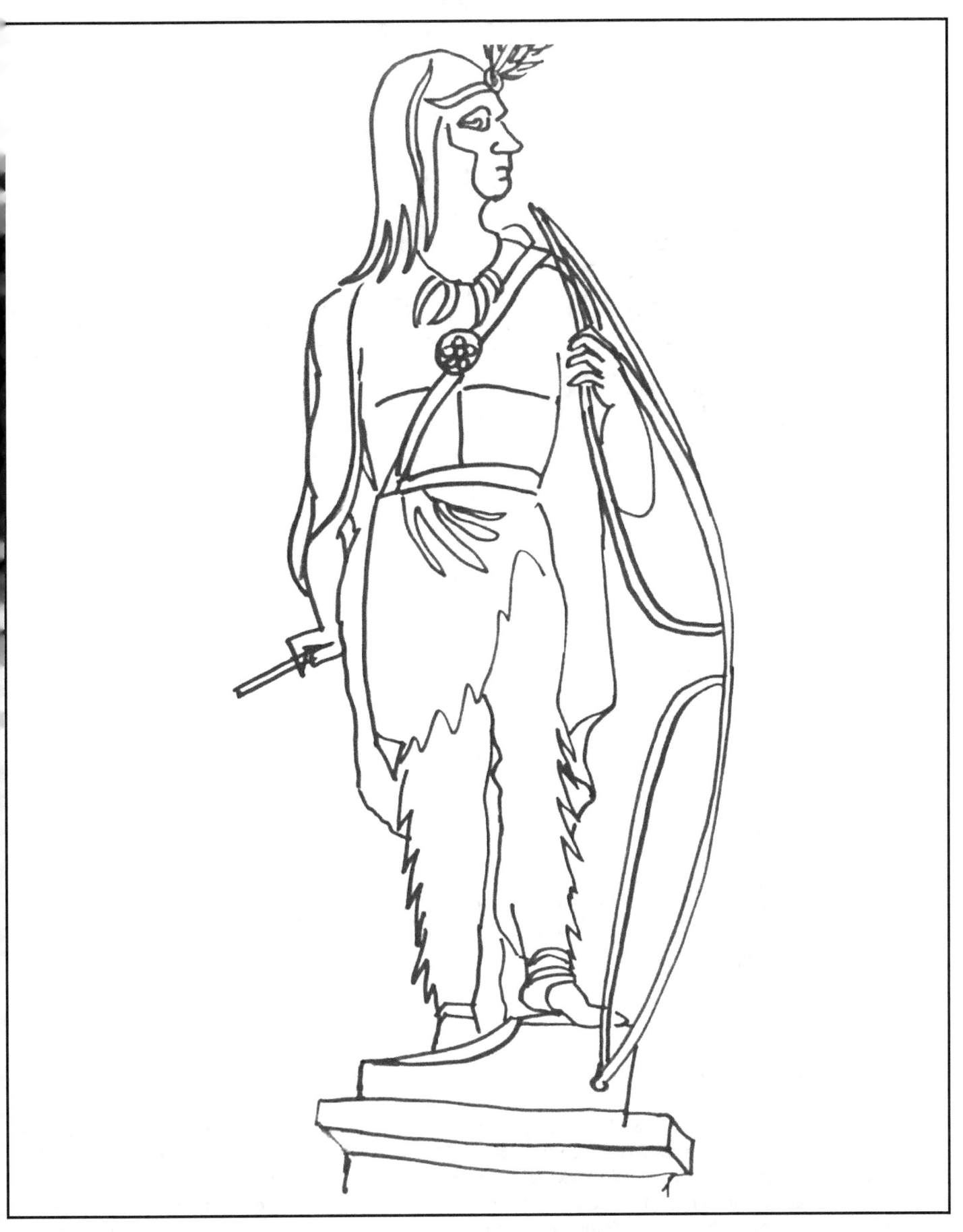

"Lawrence the Indian" was a friendly member of the Mohawk tribe that encouraged the early settlers to rebuild after the massacre of 1690. He is remembered as a bronze statue in the Stockade Historic District.

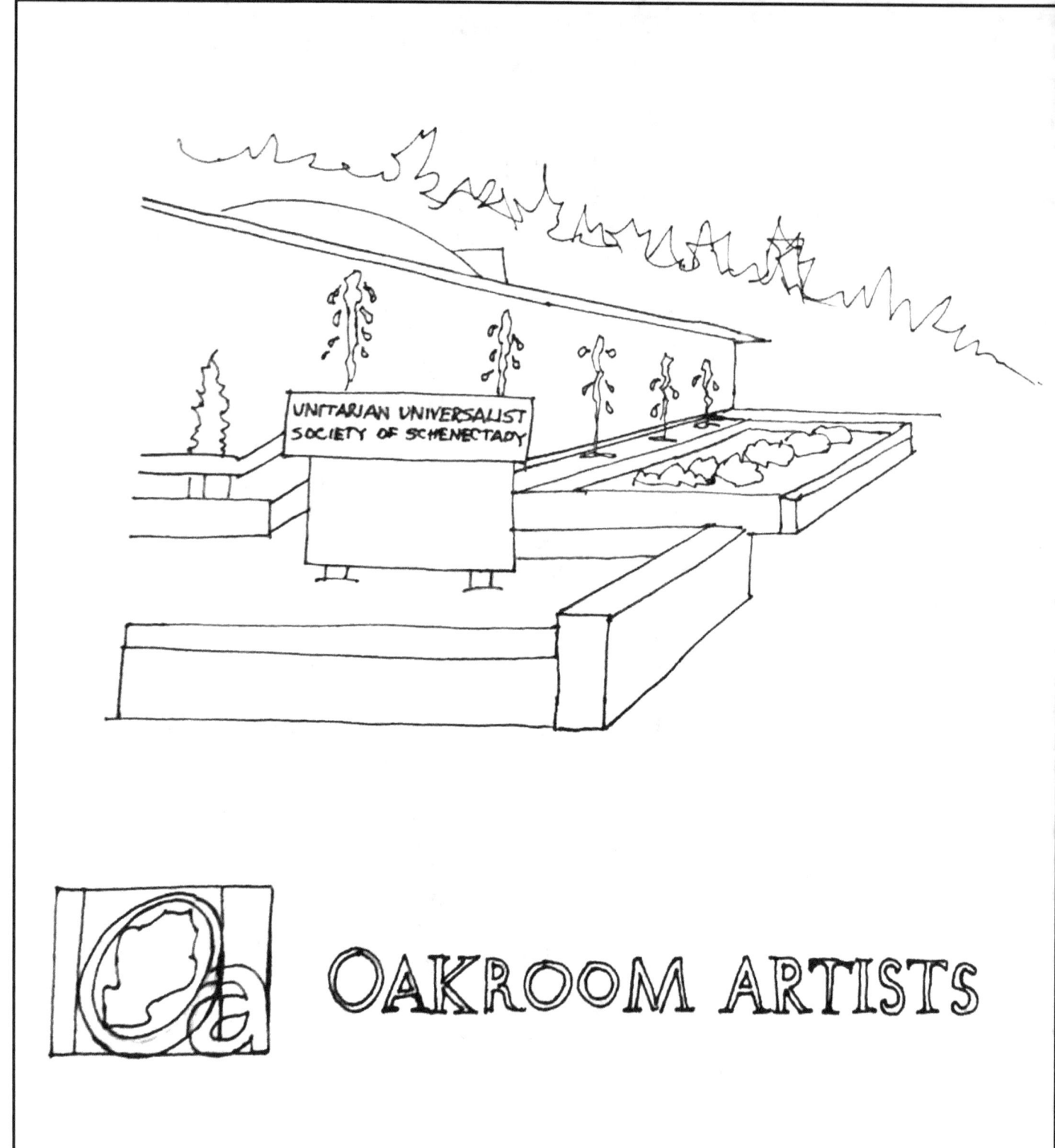

UNITARIAN UNIVERSALIST
SOCIETY OF SCHENECTADY

OAKROOM ARTISTS

The Unitarian Universalist Society was designed by famous architect Edward Durell Stone, (an early proponent of modern architecture and the associate architect for the Museum of Modern Art in NYC) and completed in 1961. It is homebase to the 60 year old Oakroom Artists. Located on Wendell Avenue in the historic GE Realty Plot. Its dominant feature is the Great Hall, an amphitheater which steps downward in circular benches as the 60-foot dome rises above it. In addition to its religious functions, the 300-seat Great Hall often serves as dramatic stage, recital hall, dance platform, art museum and lecture rostrum. The society has a history of commitment to social justice and the open exchange of ideas. Over the past century it has contained a microcosm of American liberal thought and change in a way that few other institutions in Schenectady have.

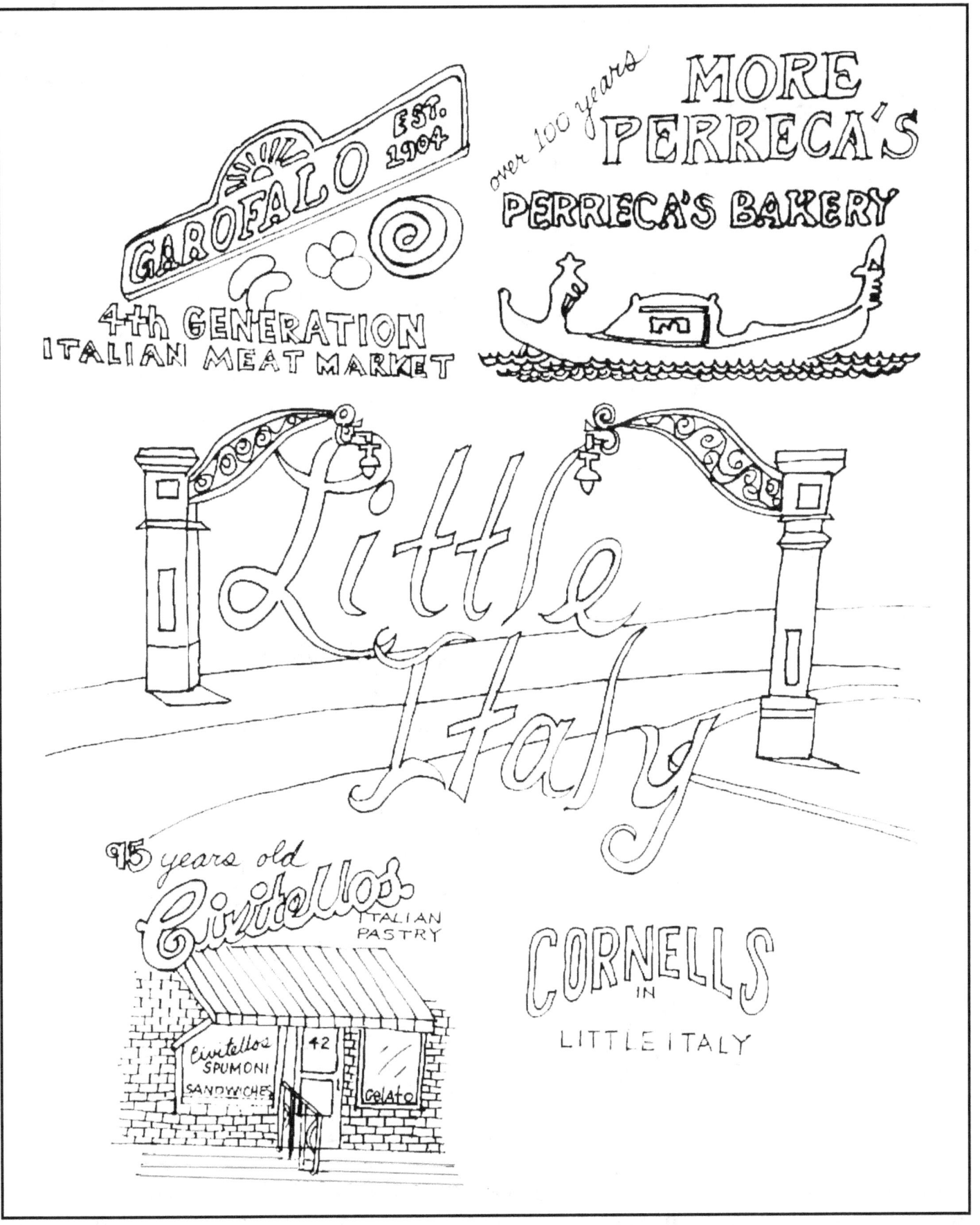

Little Italy on Jay St. has long been a fixture in Schenectady. Several of the shops have been open over 100 years. From world famous Perrecas bread, the best meats at Garafalos, Civitello's delicious cookies, fine dining at Cornell's to their yearly street fest, Little Italy is truly a gem.

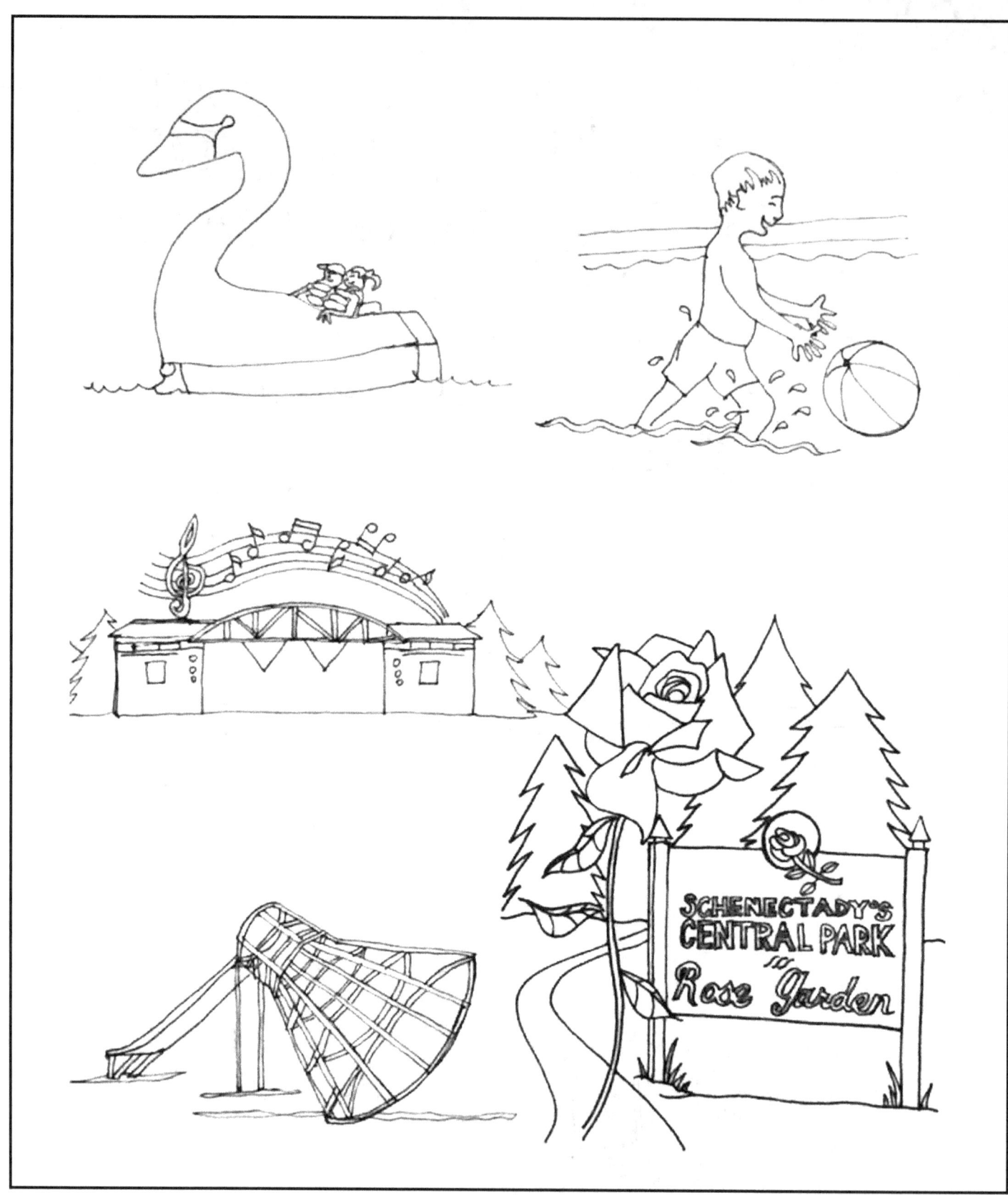

Central Park is a big beautiful park that delights visitors with a 4000 strong rose bush collection tended by the Rose Garden Restoration Committee, Iroquois Lake where you can enjoy human-powered swan boat rides, picnic grounds, concerts at Agnes McDonald Music Haven, a public pool, playgrounds and walking trails, a tennis court (turned dog park) and a community garden program hosted by the Horticulture Education Center. Due to safety reasons, they have recently removed playground equipment like the one pictured bottom left designed to look like a spaceship to commemorate the space program (which we played on countless times!)

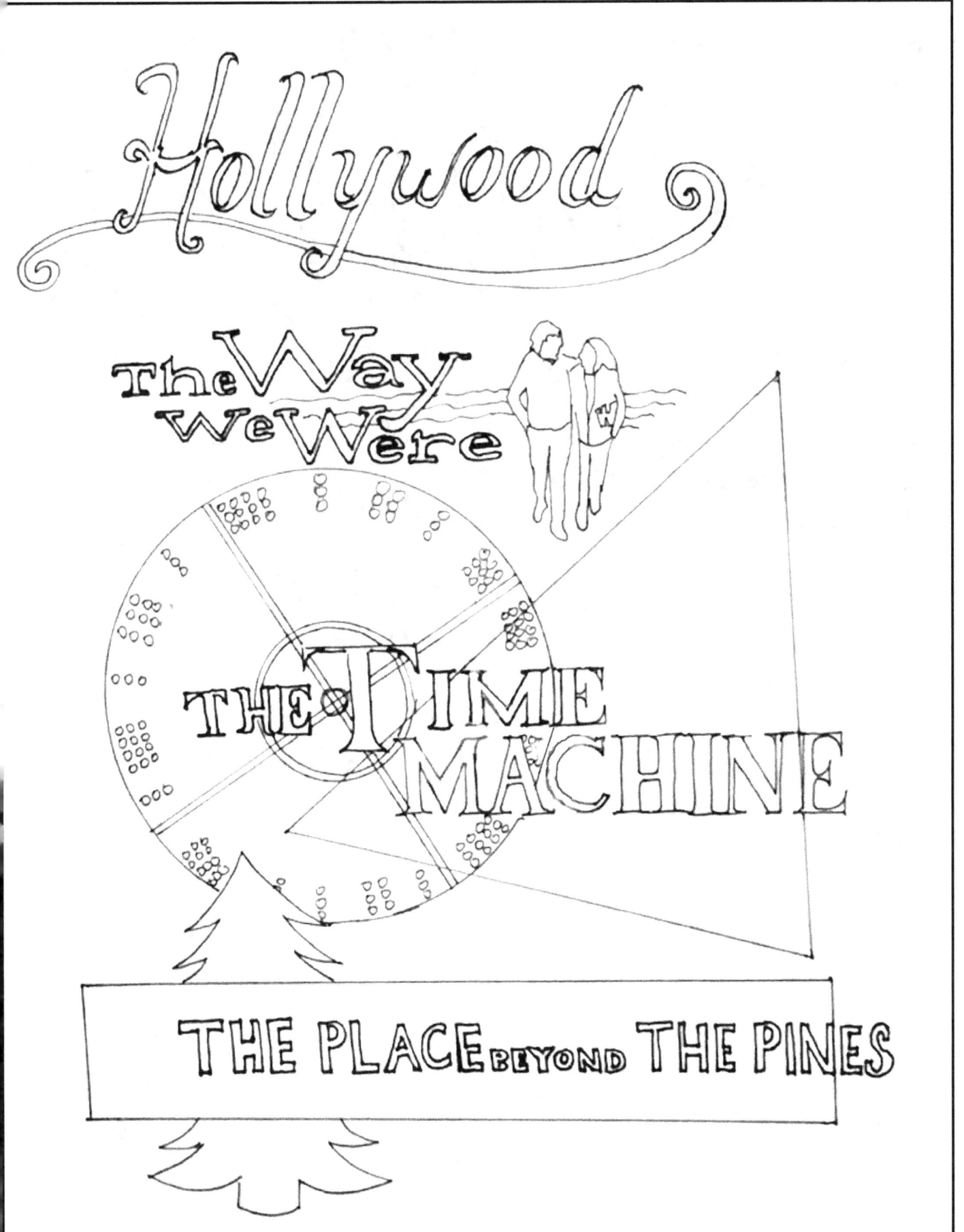

Hollywood is continually drawn to this area because of its history and architecture.

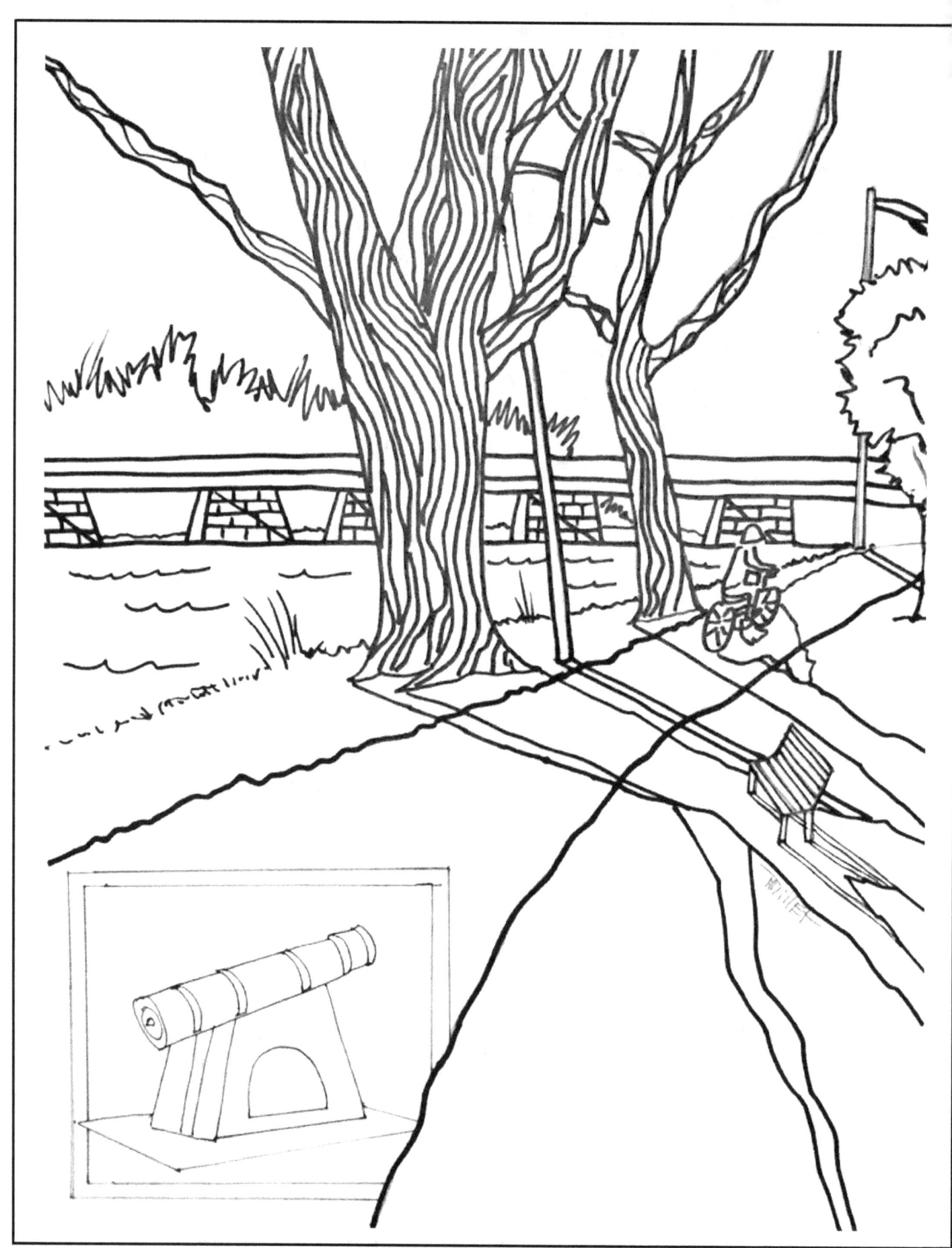

Riverside Park is a quaint peaceful park between the Stockade and the Mohawk River for walking and bike riding. An original cannon (whose age I don't know) sits facing the Mohawk.

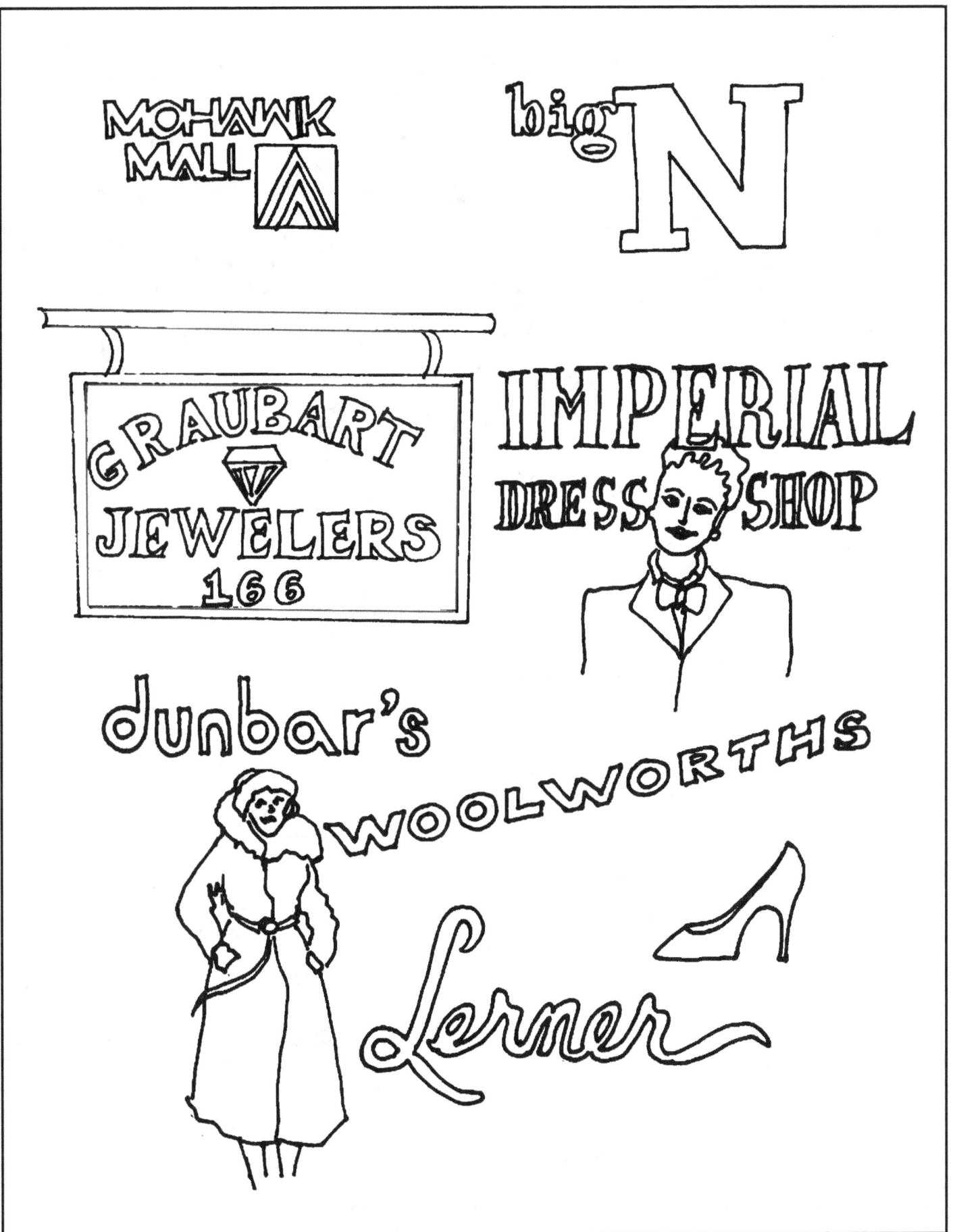

A few of the bygone popular shopping destinations in Schenectady.

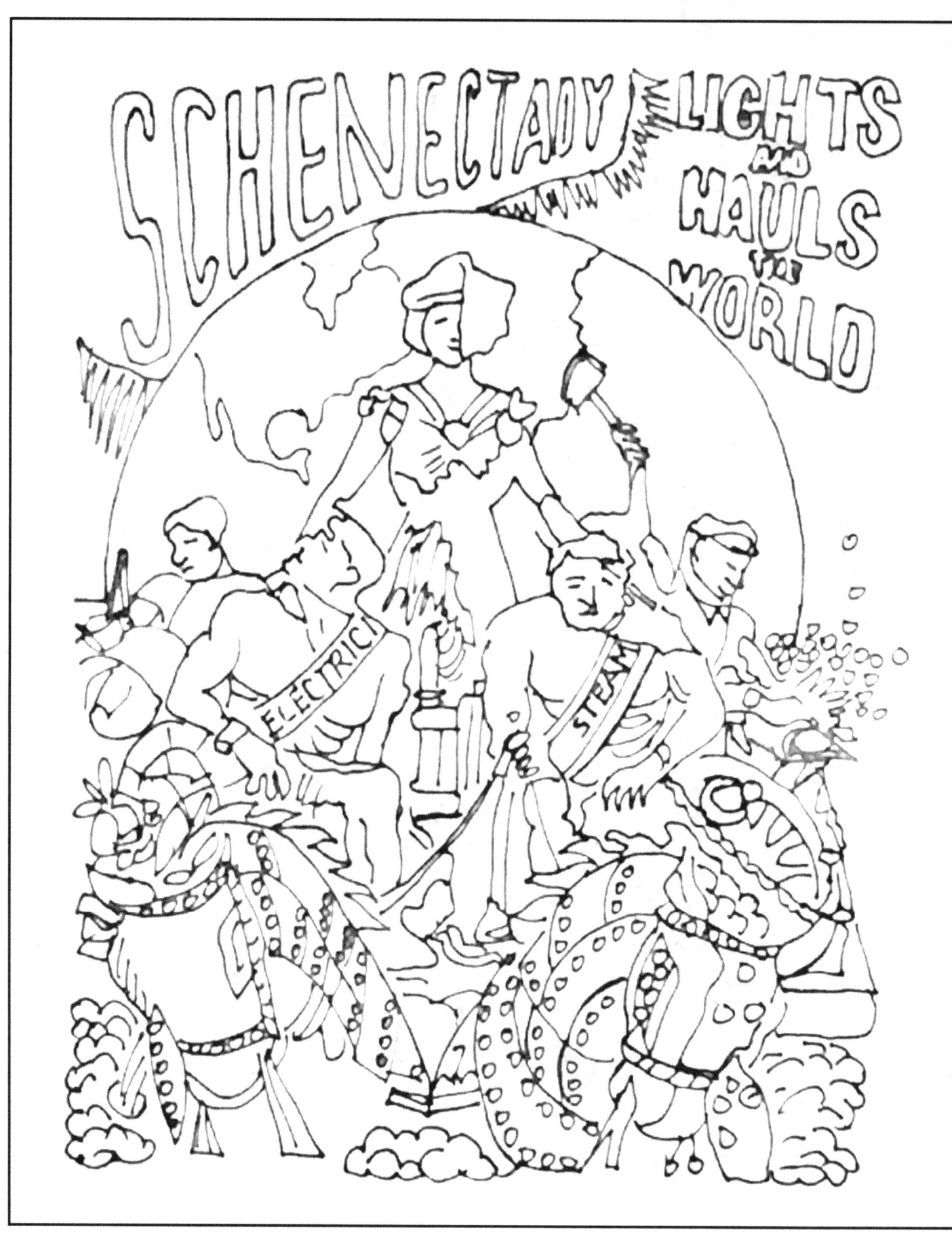

"Schenectady Lights and Hauls the World" was coined as a phrase referring to the twin industries of Schenectady, electricity and locomotives. Augustus Crouse was the crafter of this fine illustration in 1910.

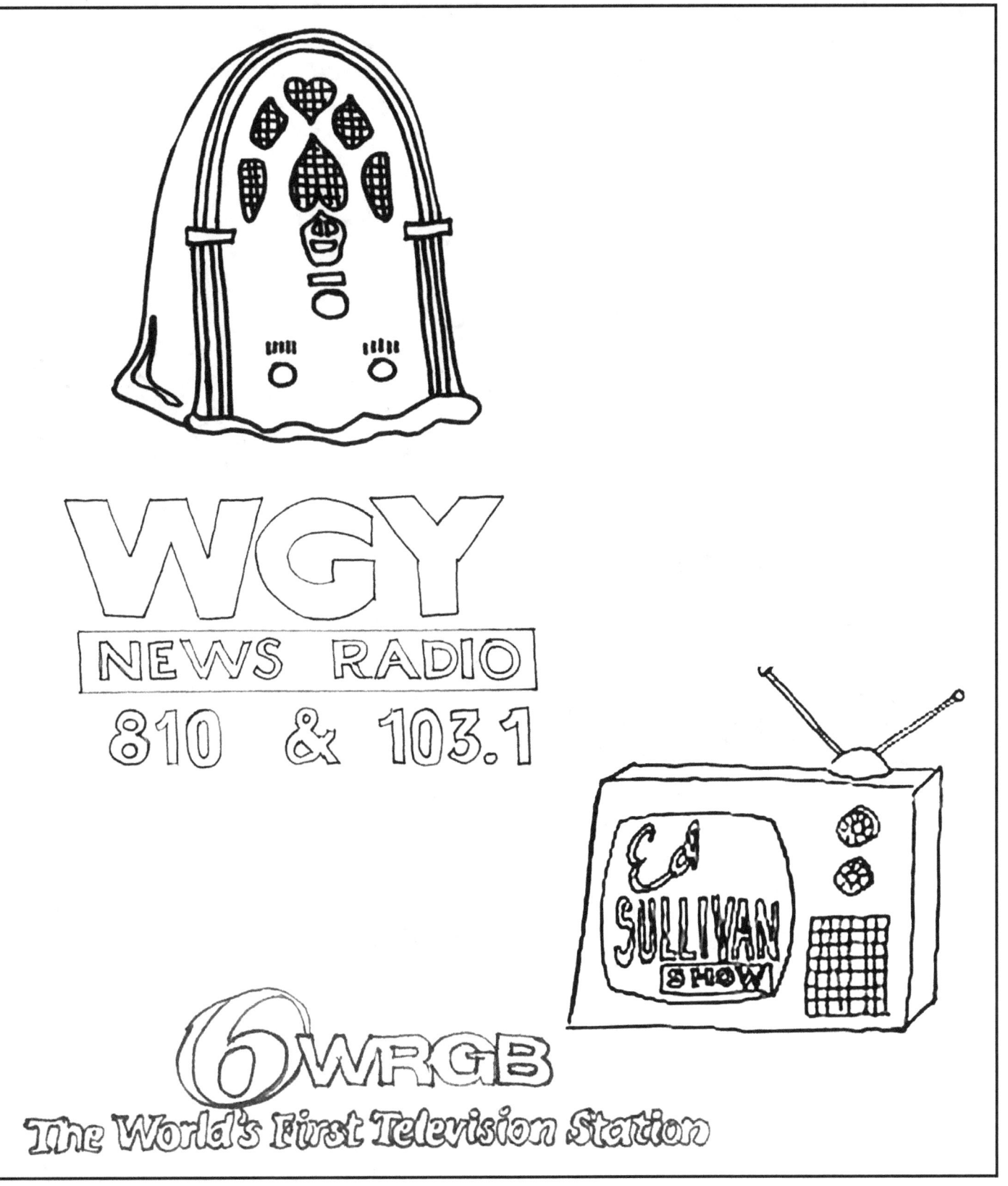

WGY radio is one of the oldest stations in the U.S. Having begun broadcasting in 1922. KH Hager signed on at Building 36 at GE explaining that the W stood for wireless, the G stood for General Electric and the Y stood for Schenectady. In the same year, Edward H Smith directed the first radio drama and became the first Foley (reproduction of everyday sounds such as slamming 2x4s together to simulate a slamming door) artist as well. WGY also pioneered remote broadcasting with a concert at Union College and the first condenser microphone.

WRGB is the first experimental television station in the world. It began broadcasting in 1928.

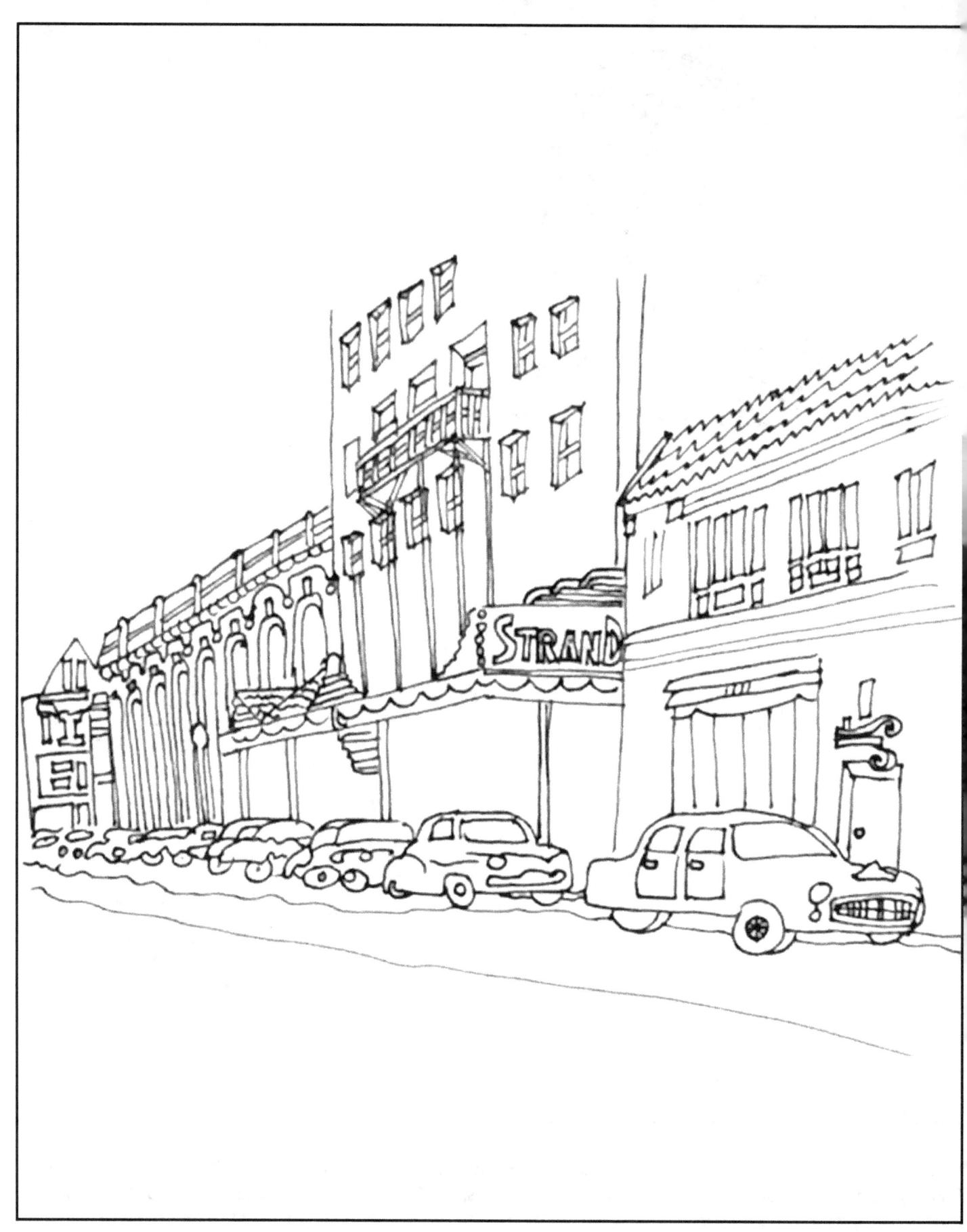

The Strand Theater was originally opened as the Orpheum Theatre prior to 1908, and then renamed Palace Theatre. The Strand Theatre, located on State Street, is notable for being the first Schenectady movie house to screen a "talking picture", Al Jolson's "The Jazz Singer" in 1927.

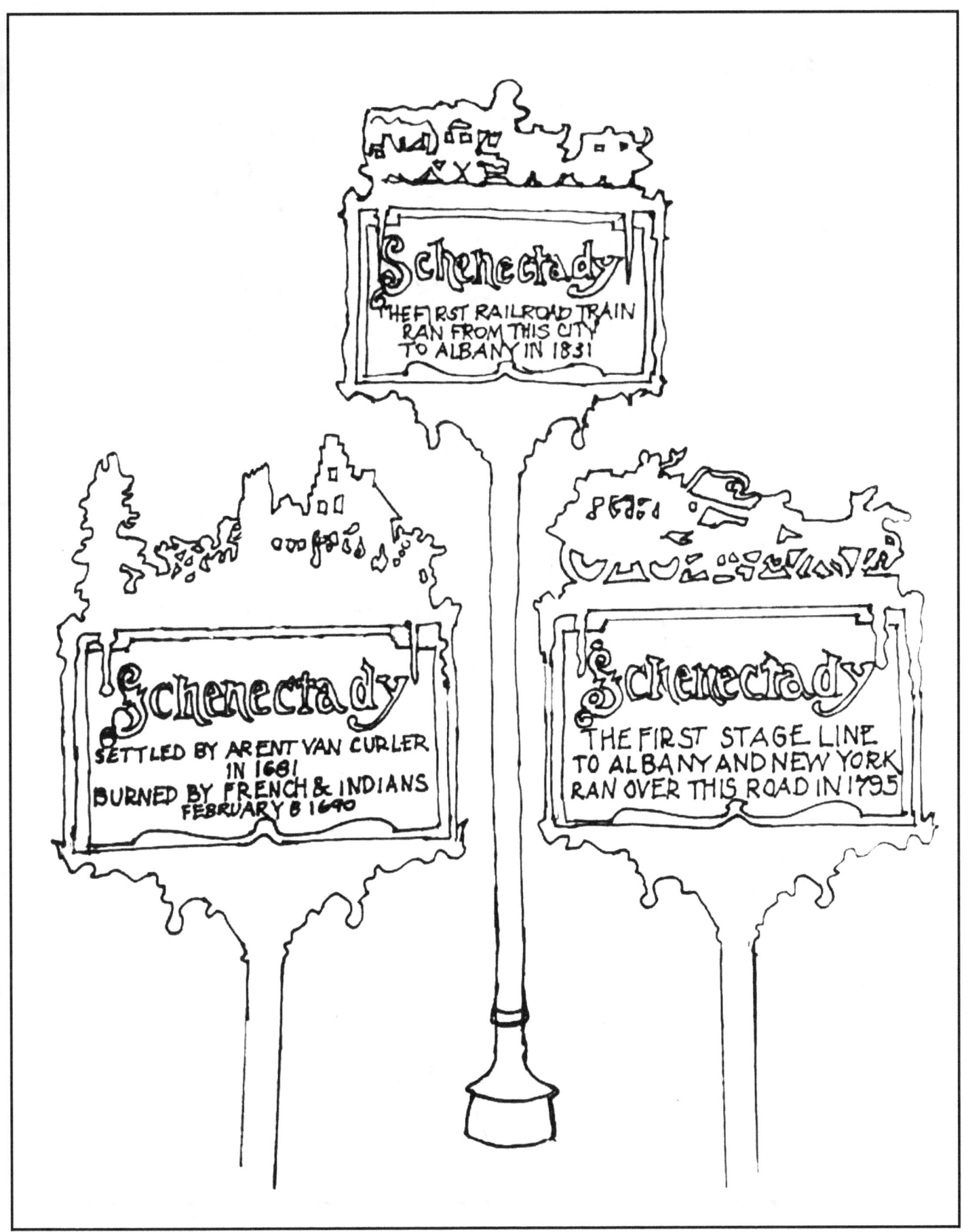

The 3 Schenectady signs that were made to commemorate the settling, burning, and rebuilding of Schenectady, the first stage line to Albany and New York and the first railroad train in 1831.

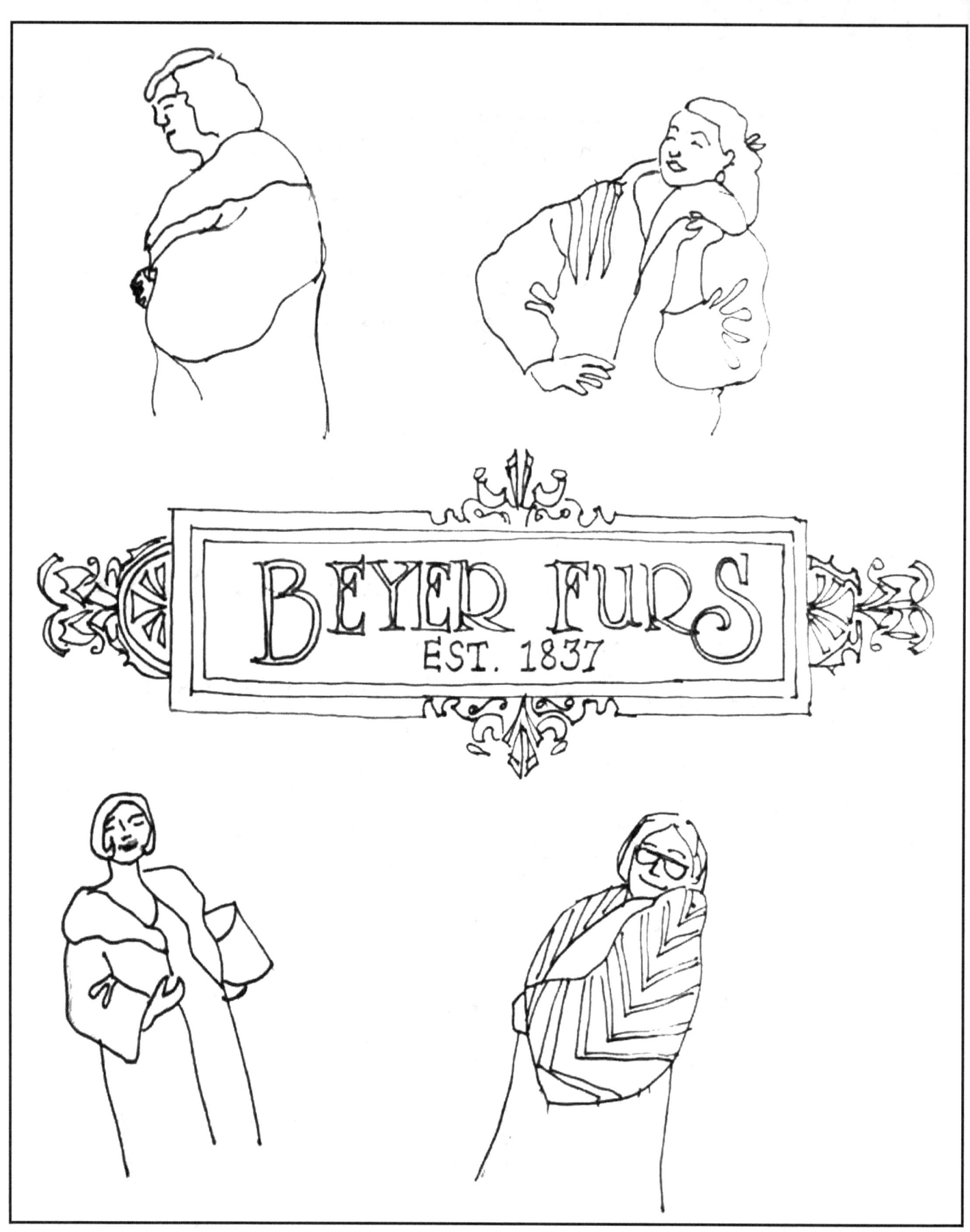

Tri-City's oldest business, Beyer Furs has been keeping us warm since 1837. Now based at 1408 Union St., Christa still repairs, cleans and restores many different types of furs.

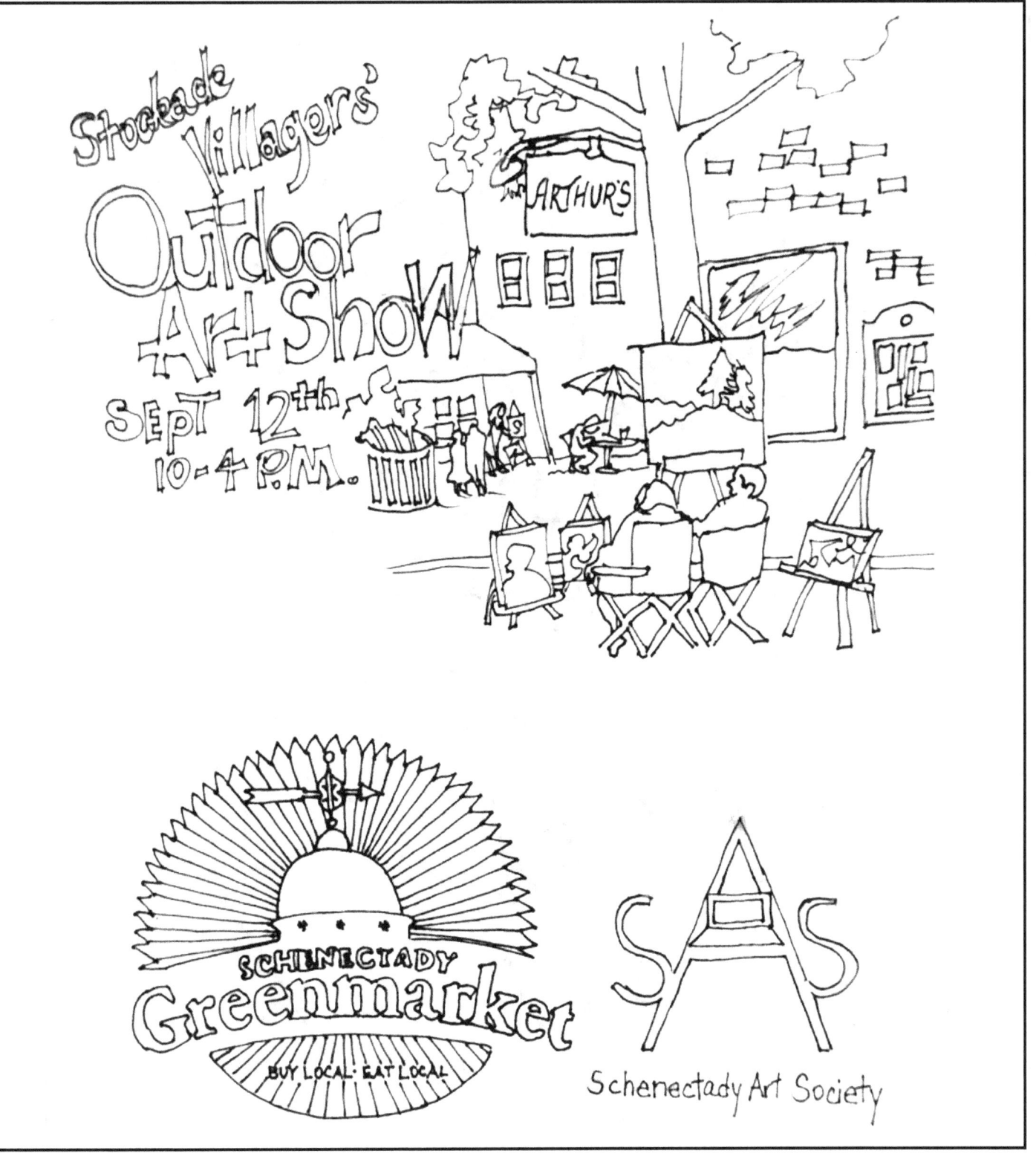

Two popular long standing outdoor markets are depicted here. The Stockade Villagers Art Show, held in the Stockade Historic District, has showcased the rich talent in this area in September for 65 years.

The Greenmarket farmers market has occurred every Sunday surrounding City Hall since 2000 and moves indoors to Proctors in the winter.

The Schenectady Art Society was founded in 1967. Their purpose is to encourage local artists by offering educational programs and opportunities to exhibit and sell their work to the community.

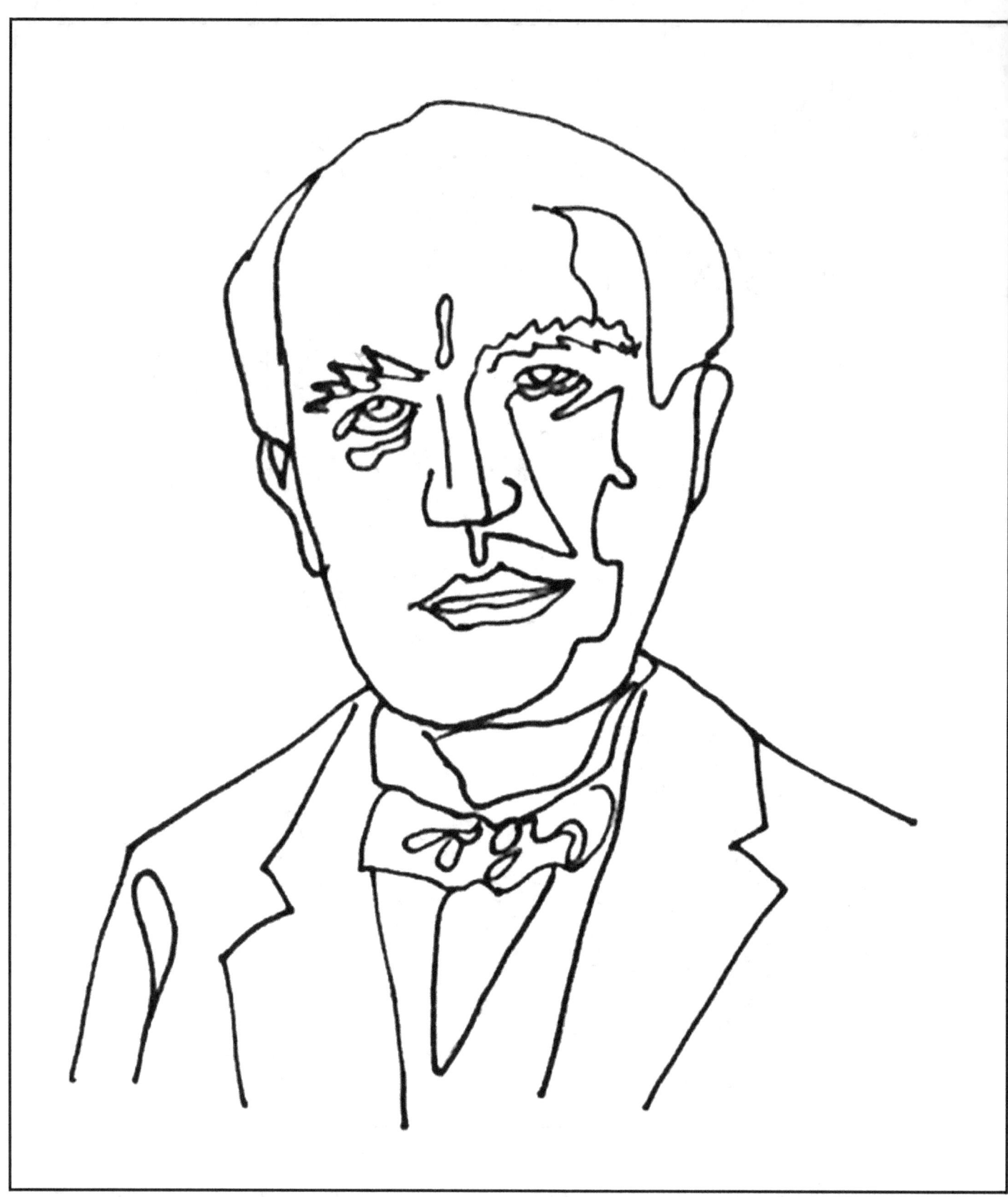

Thomas Alva Edison, moved his Edison Machine Works from Menlo Park, NJ to Schenectady in 1887 where it became General Electric. He was responsible for many inventions including the phonograph in 1878, the motion picture camera and perfecting the incandescent light bulb in 1879 to name a few of his 1,093 patents. He revolutionized mass communication by inventing the recording and reproduction of sound and ushered in the era of "talking pictures". Amazing since he was deaf! He also created the first lab devoted to scientific research.

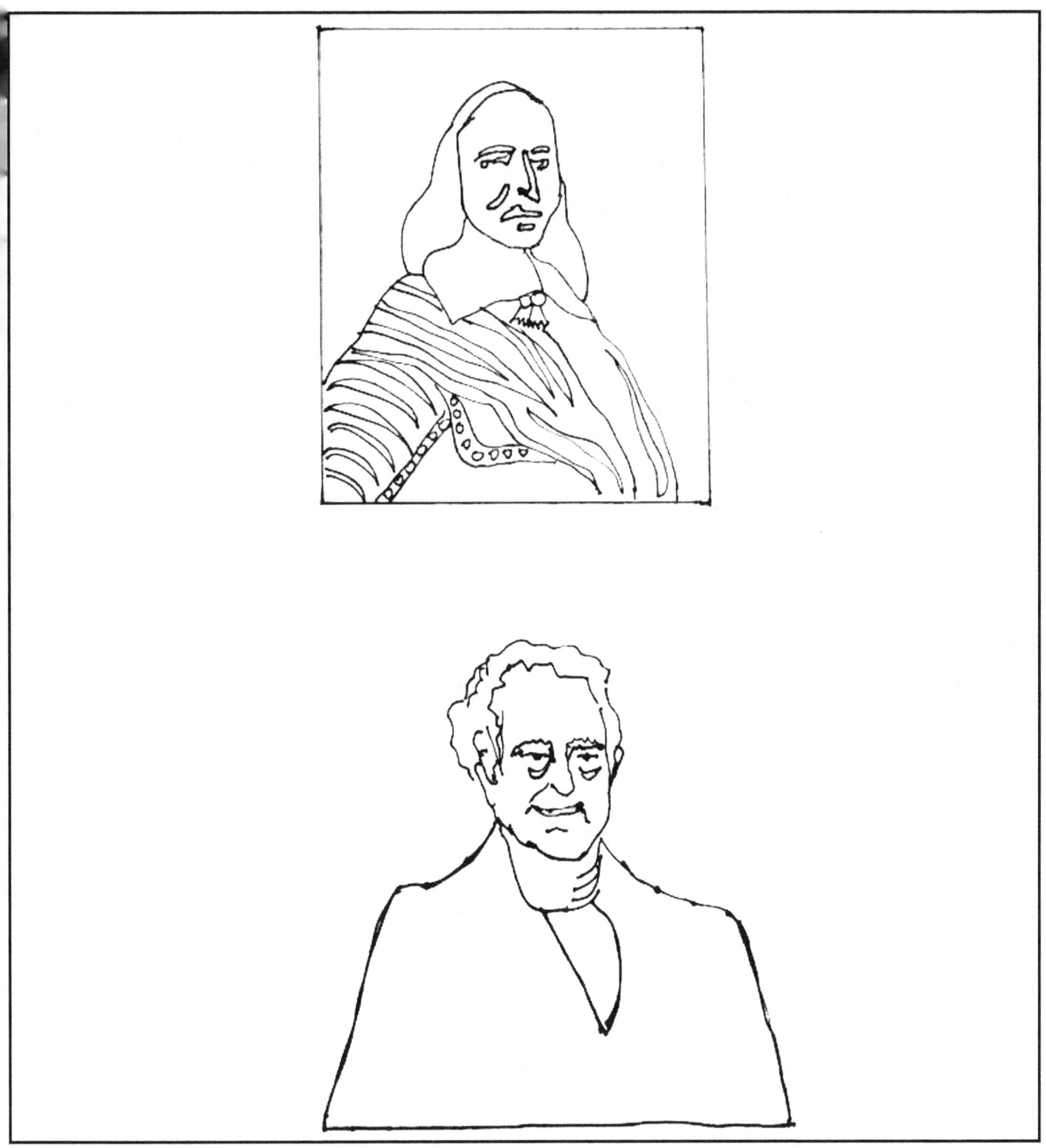

Arendt Van Curler founded the city of Schenectady in 1662. He purchased the land from the Mohawks and was known for his fair dealings with them, negotiating disputes and arranging for captives to be freed. His home is now the Stockade Inn which was originally built in 1814 for the Mohawk Bank, the first bank in Schenectady.

Eliphalet Nott, born in 1773, became a minister, educational pioneer and scientist who studied heat and obtained some thirty or more patents for applications of heat to steam engines. He was best known in his day as the inventor of the first stove for anthracite coal, which was named for him. In 1804 he became president of Union, at the age of 31 and continued until his death in 1866. He remains the longest serving college president in the country. The Nott Memorial is named for him as well as Nott St and Nott Terrace.

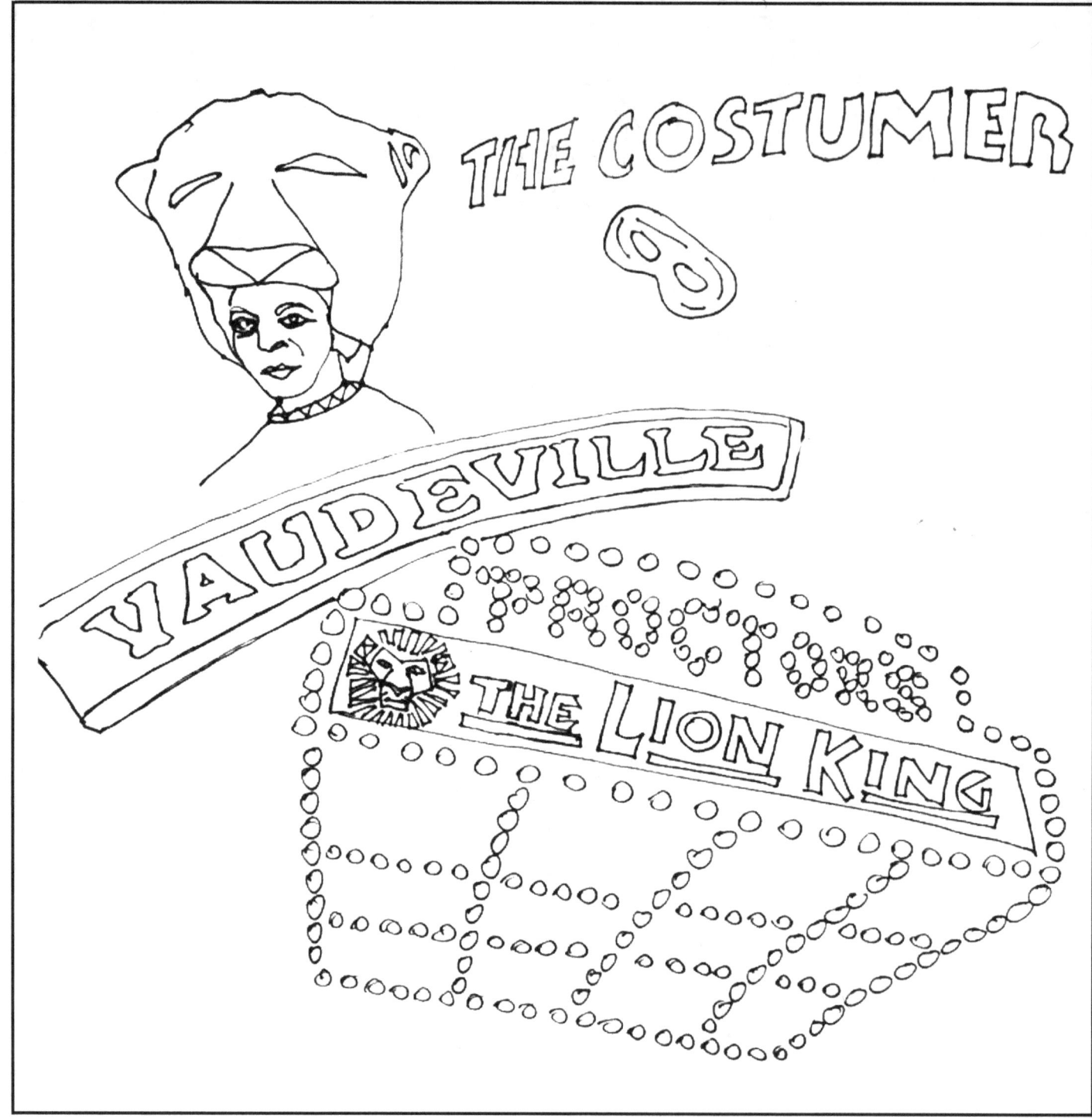

Two icons of entertainment in town are The Costumer and Proctors.

The Costumer, which turns 100 next year is a vast warehouse that supplies costumes and accessories worldwide. Housed in two locations, it is the go-to place year round for any way you might want to dress up. Pictured here is my daughter in law, Jessica Westervelt, who works for the Costumer, dressed up in full Lion King regalia for the Costumer's catalog.

Proctors Theater has been around since 1926 from the days of vaudeville. It hosts world renowned Broadway shows, plays, cutting edge film festivals and events. In 1930, Proctors hosted the first public demonstration of television with the help of General Electric. Proctors is the grande dame of Schenectady, a dazzling old hall of gilt embellishments, elegant balconies and old world charm. It is as much a vision to behold as the shows it offers.

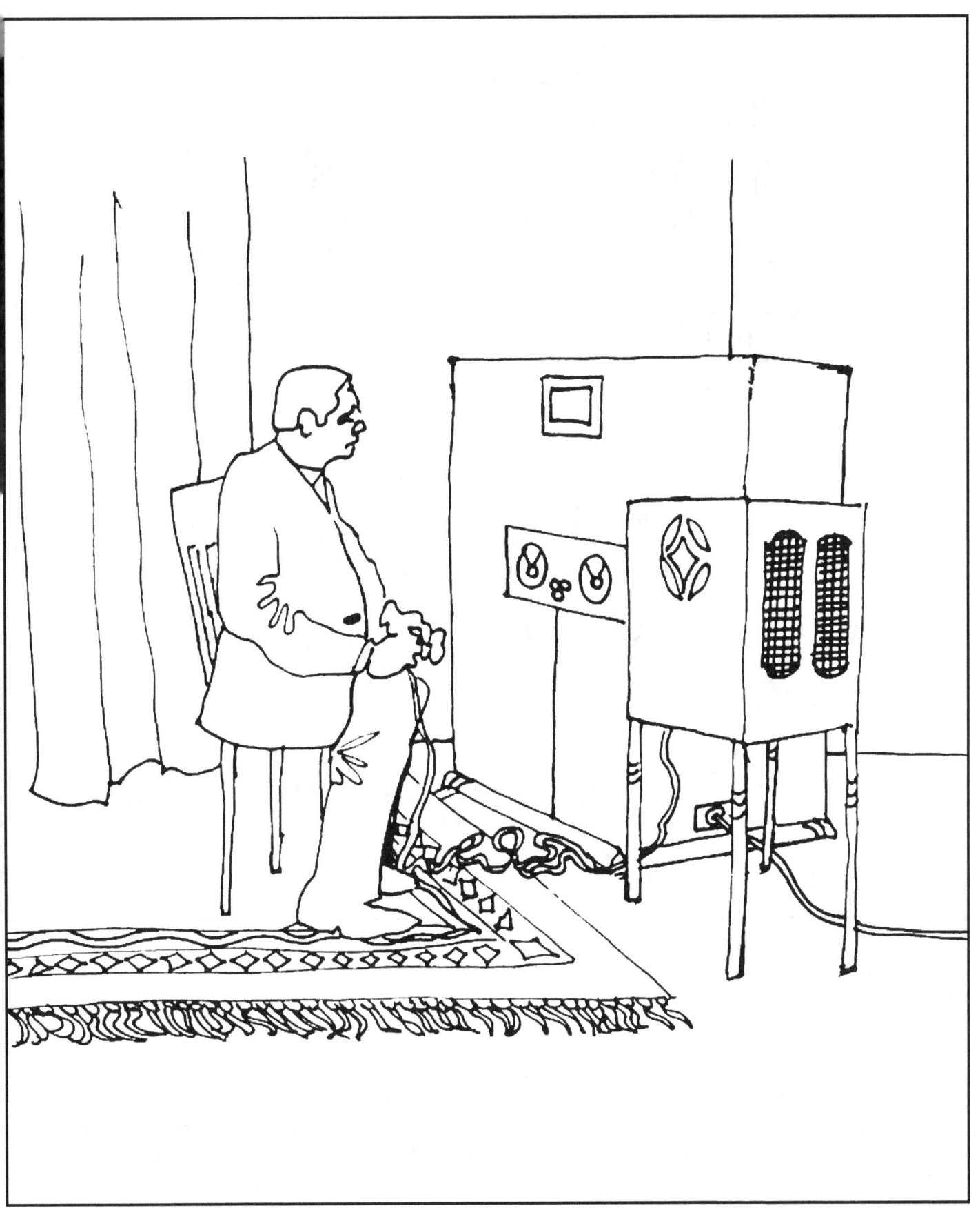

Dr. Ernst Alexanderson, a Swedish electrical engineer who worked for GE, broadcast the first televised drama in 1927 on a 3"X 3" screen at his home on Adams St in the GE Realty Plot (a tract of land specifically for GE executives). In addition to designing the Alexanderson alternator, an early long wave radio transmitter, he received 345 patents, the last filed in 1968 at age 89.

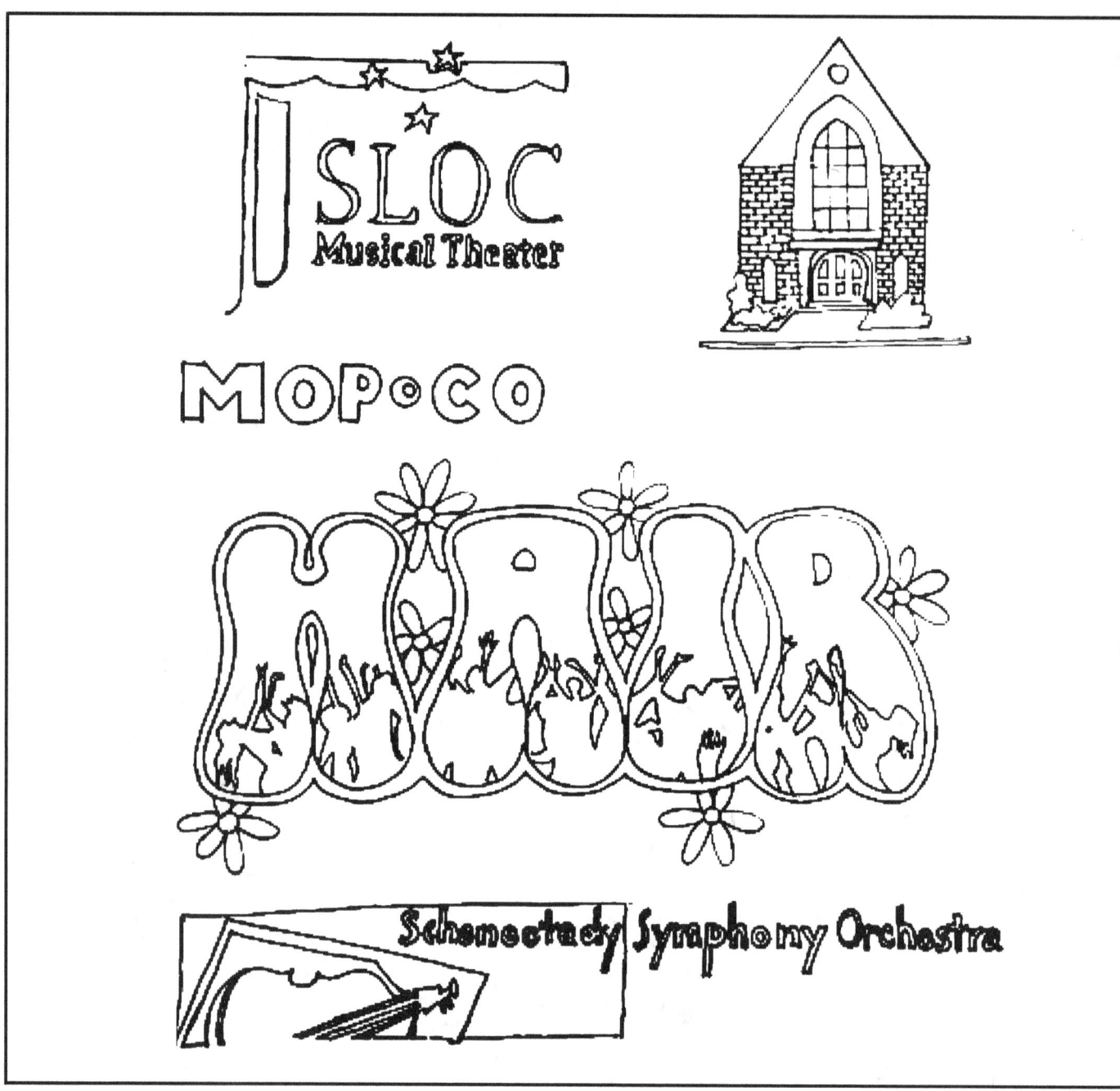

Schenectady Light Opera Company was born in 1926 when a group of Van Corlaer and Draper alumni joined together to present short plays containing songs and comedy acts. It is now performing in the old St. John the Baptist church.

The Schenectady Civic Players was founded in 1927 by Union College Educators in a former mid 19th century Masonic temple in Schenectady's historic Stockade District. It has produced almost 450 plays. Just a few years ago the Red Cross building next door was acquired to provide space for the costume collection, group activities, office and archival work. This building was built in 1869 by St George's Lodge of Masons.

Mop and Co. is a newcomer to the performing arts/theater district in town, opened in 2005. It performs, teaches and trains improv. Now in its new digs on Jay St., there is more room for exciting improvisation as a direct form of entertainment. as a personal developmental tool and as a training tool for businesses.

Schenectady Symphony Orchestra is a talented group of more than seventy musicians, working under the leadership of award-winning Music Director Charles Schneider.

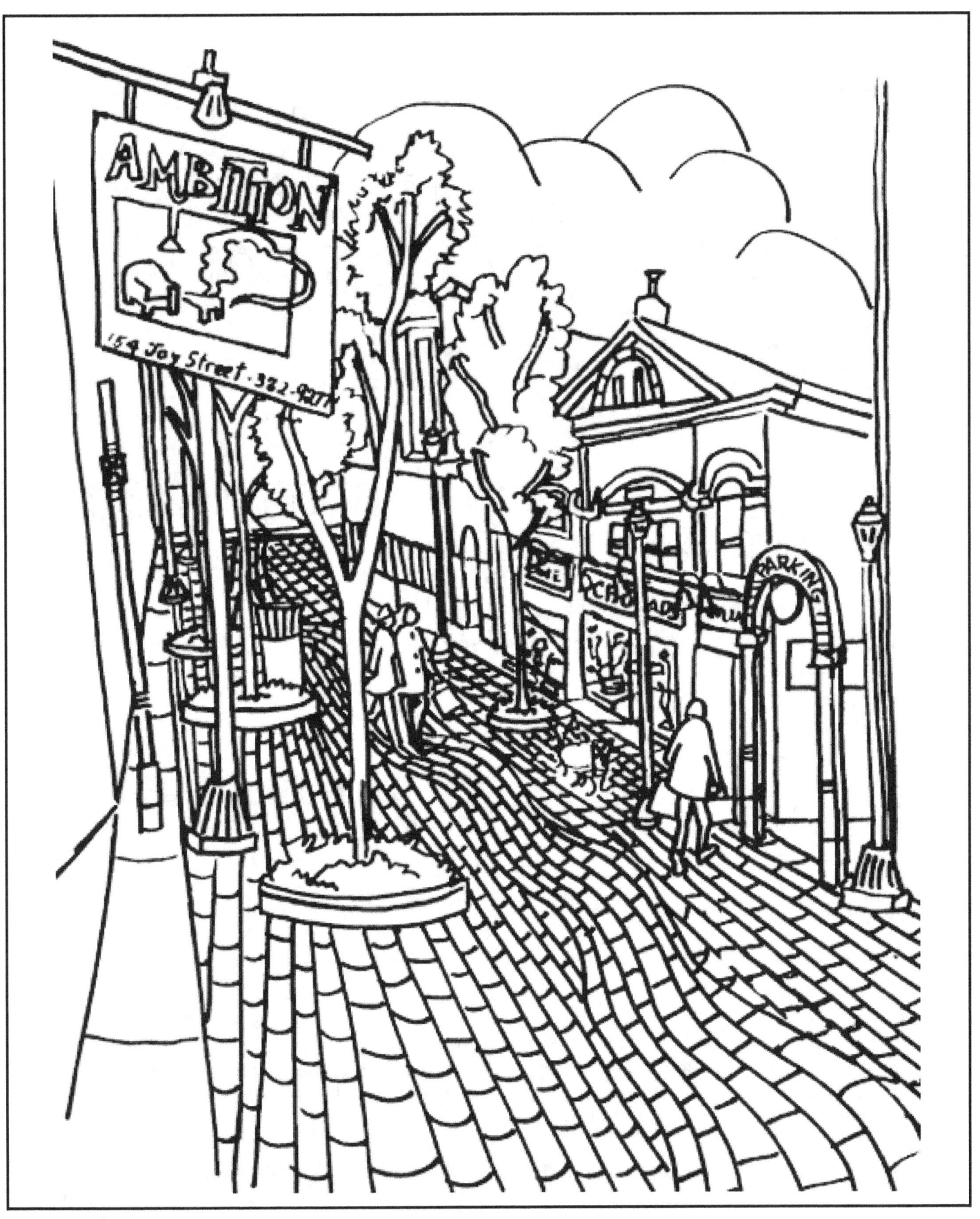

Jay St. is a quaint bohemian tree- and brick-lined pedestrian walkway where you can find unusual shops that sell a little bit of everything. Here you can get a tattoo, browse for vintage items, artisan made gifts and books, sip coffee and so much more. Some shops have resided here for decades and new ones pop up every year. Ambition café's quirky décor and great food attracts celebrities that are in town performing at Proctors theater.

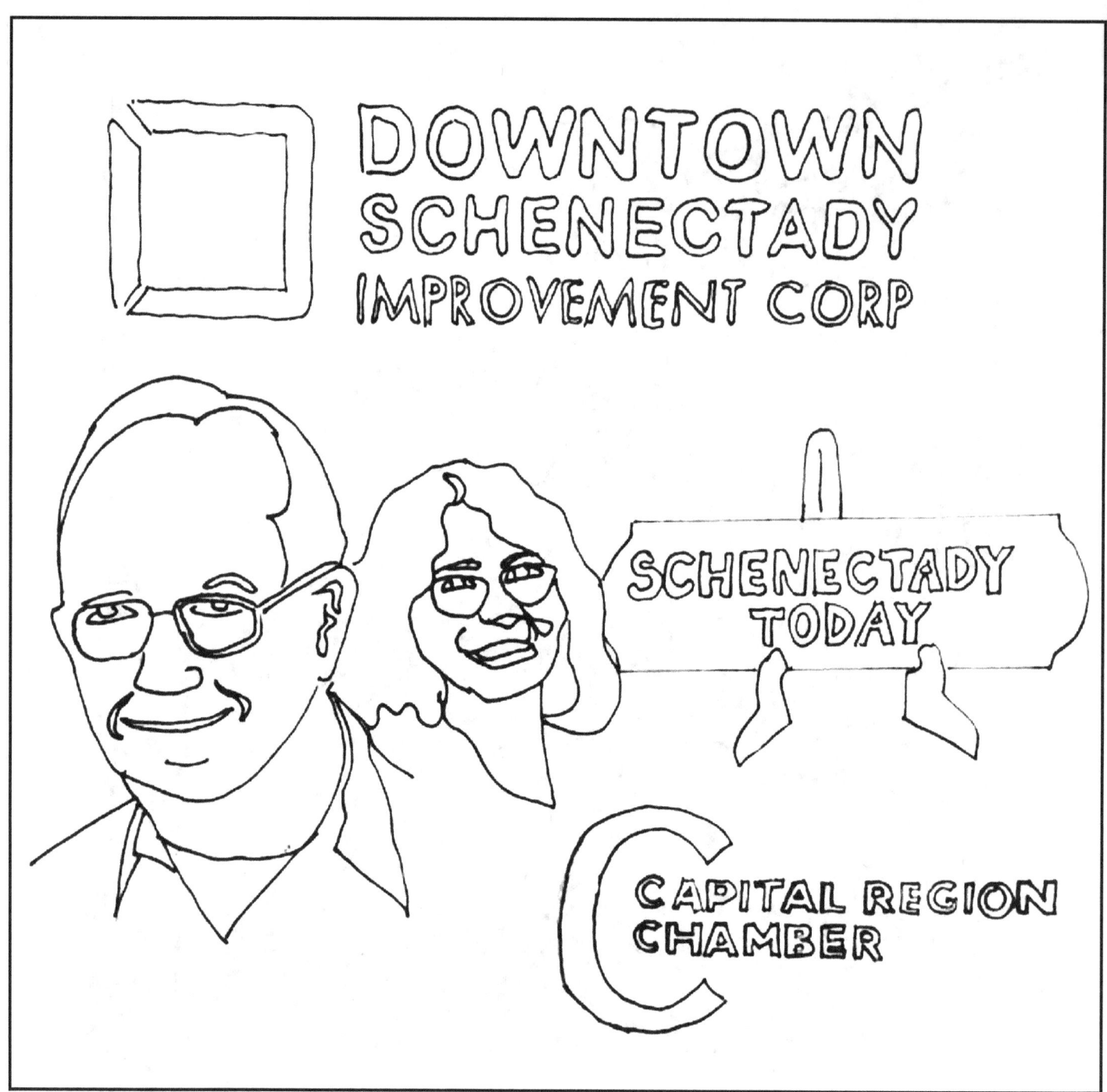

Schenectady Today is an 18 year old informative local talk show hosted by the delightful Ann Parillo and was masterfully produced by the late Gregg Millett (yes, we have discussed the possibility of being related!). Locals and celebs alike have graced their stage. Ann always has her finger on the pulse of Schenectady. Gregg was responsible for creating the Sister City project between Schenectady and Kunming, China and was the founder of Singles Outreach Services in the Capital Region.

Downtown Schenectady Improvement Corporation is the place to find out what's happening in town. They also are responsible for the visual appeal and promotion of it as a regional destination for shopping, dining, recreation and living. They also house the IRS Small Business and Self-Employed Tax Center and the NYS Small Business Development Center.

The Capital Region Chamber is the hub of business serving Albany, Schenectady and Troy. They work tirelessly to help you expand your network and grow your business!

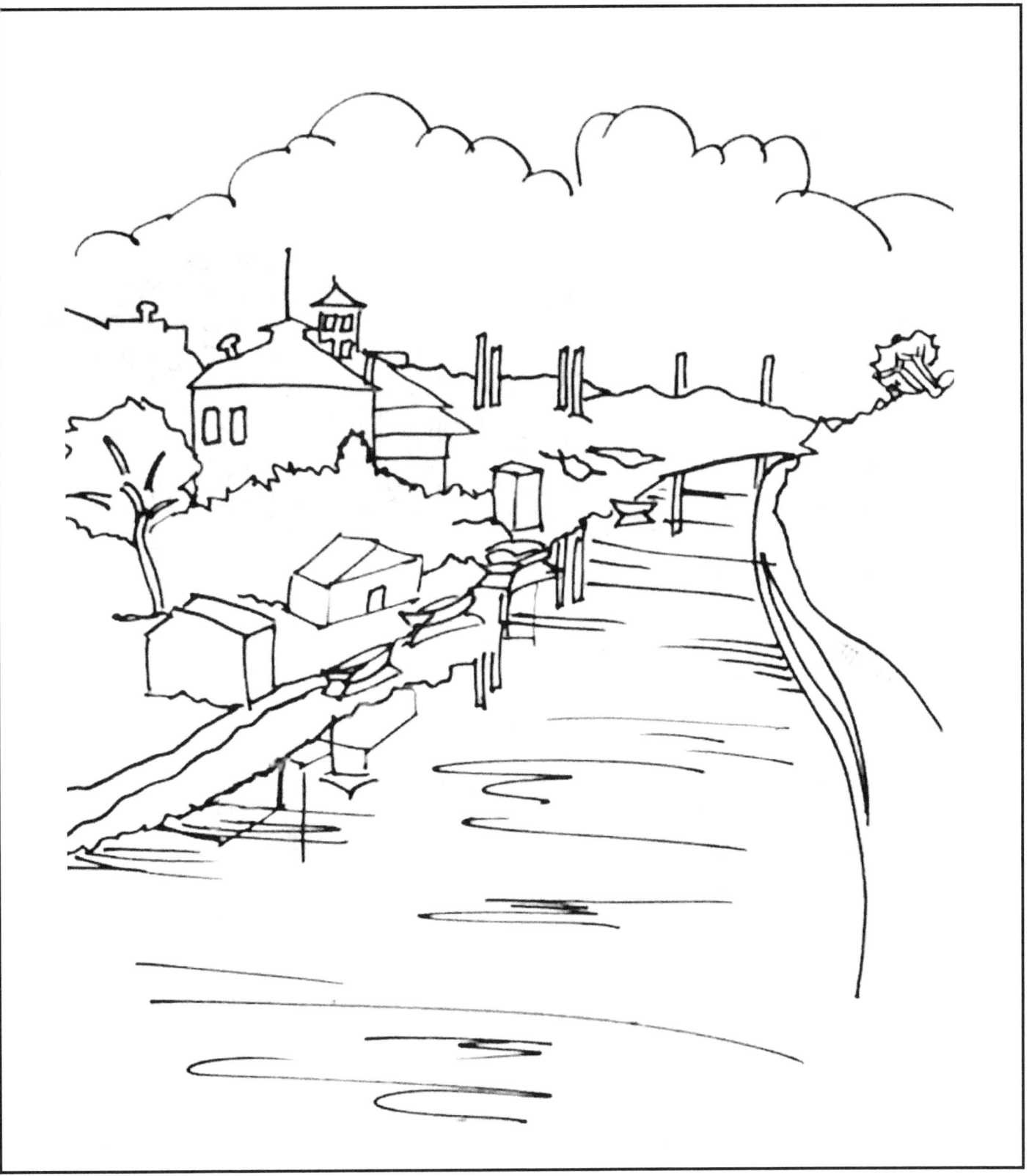

The Erie Canal was an engineering marvel. Some called it the Eighth Wonder of the World. Consisting of 363 miles from Albany to Buffalo, building began in 1817 and opened in 1835. Nicknamed Clintons Big Ditch, DeWitt Clinton planned the first transportation system between the Eastern Seaboard and the western interior of the U.S. that did not require portage. In 2000, it was recognized as the most successful human built waterway and most important work of civil engineering in North America. It was filled in in 1925 in Schenectady and water traffic was moved to the Mohawk River because it was too narrow and shallow for the bigger boats to navigate. Vestiges of it can still be seen on what is now called Erie Blvd.

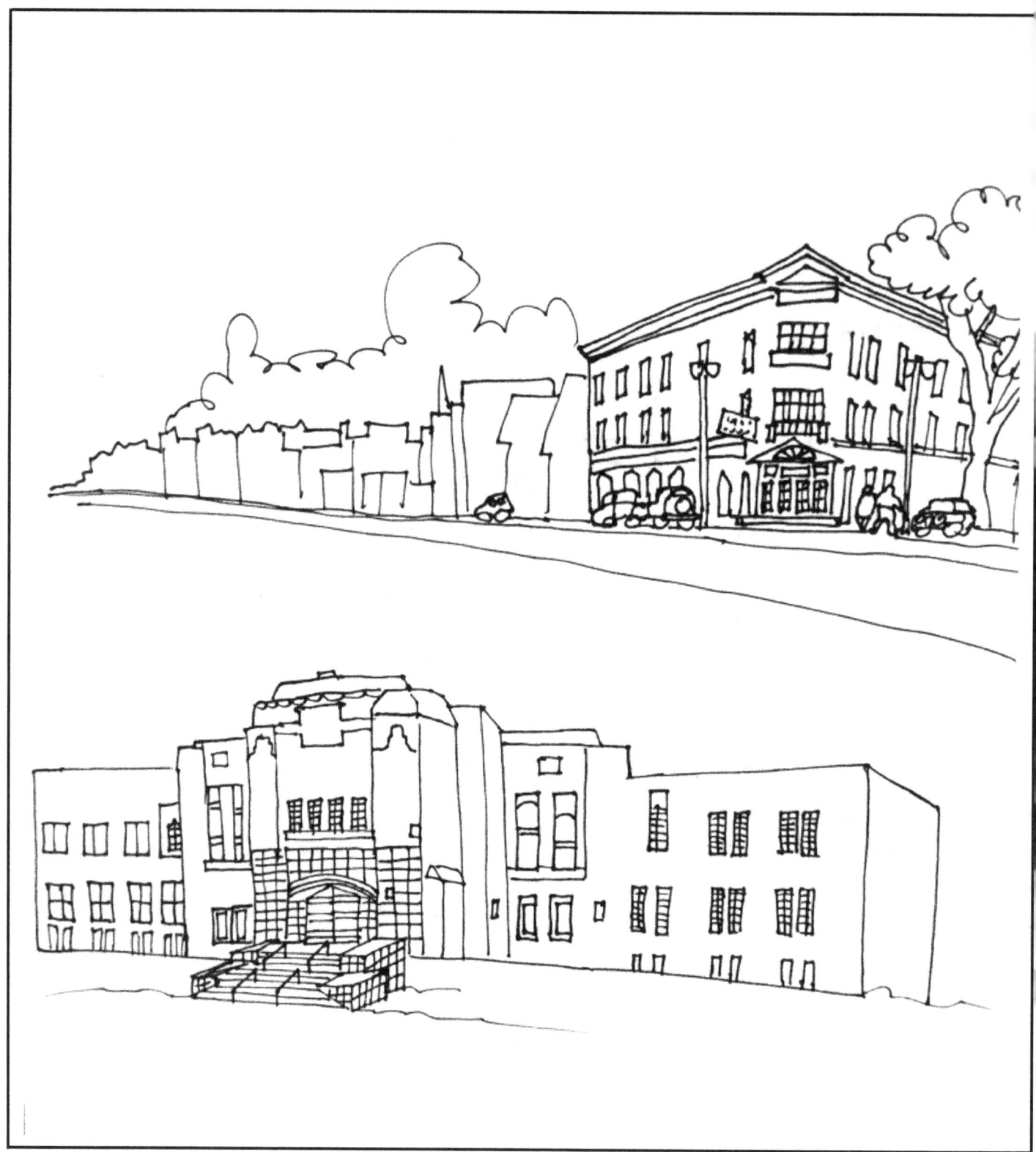

My grandfather, Gus Flynn, owned the Roosevelt Hotel where the Armory now stands. Infamous celebrities like Legs Diamond and his mistress would stay there while in town. Our family history is rich with stories of how fine jewelry was passed over the bar to pay for drinks during the Depression.

The massive Armory, built in 1936, was designed by New York's state architect at that time, William Haugaard. It is a combination of Art Deco and "Tudorbethan" styles. The armory remains virtually intact today. It was home to two units of the New York Army National Guard until it was closed in 2008. In 1995 it was listed on the National Register of Historic Places. It now sponsors sporting events and more.

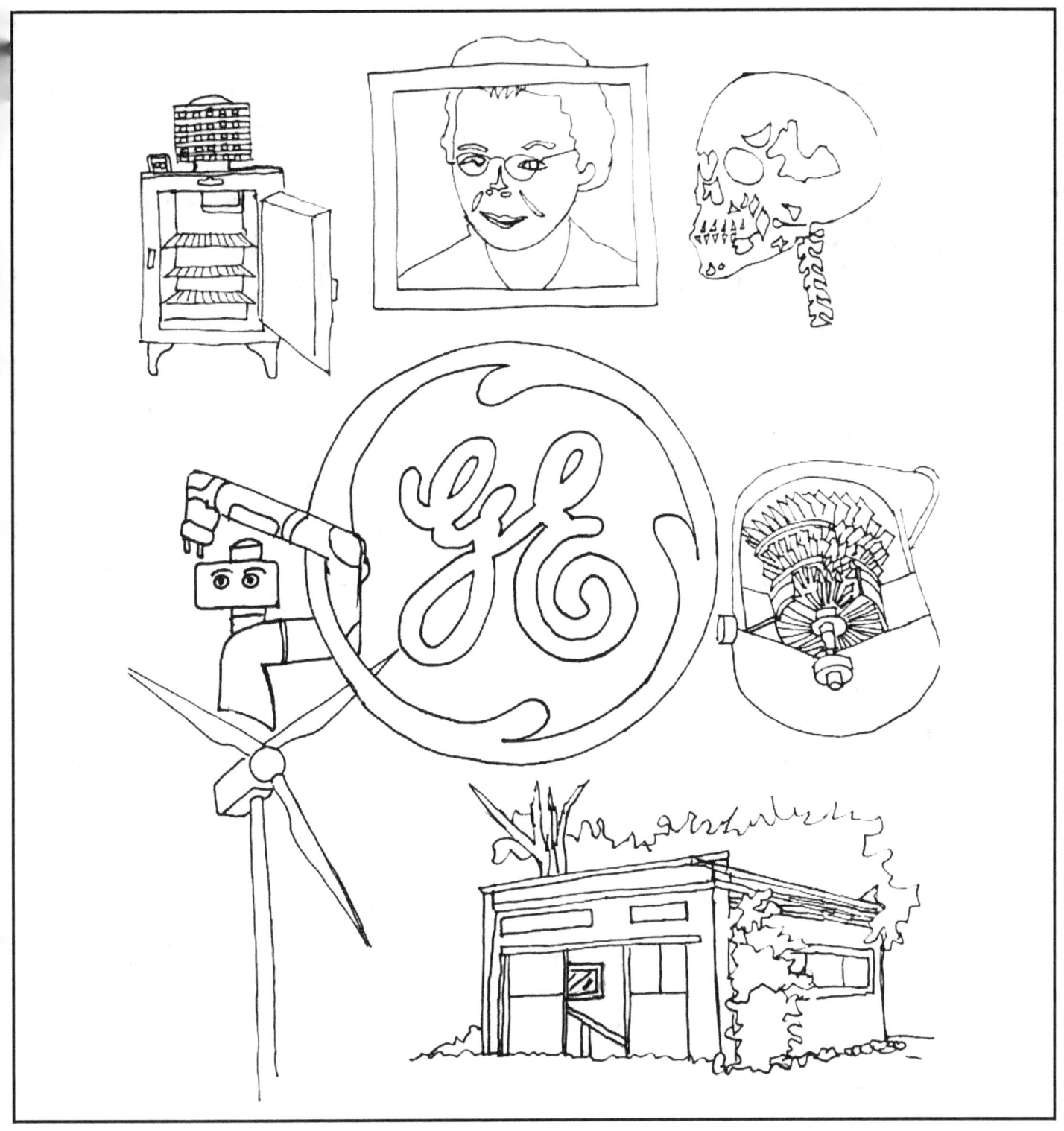

No coloring book of Schenectady would be complete without mentioning GE. Thomas Edison began the Edison Machine Works in Menlo Park, NJ in 1881. He moved it to Schenectady and eventually it became General Electric in 1892. GE's contributions to the world are too vast to mention in this small space, not to mention putting Schenectady on the map. In addition to "talking pictures", television and radio and so much more, GE revolutionized refrigeration with the monitor top pictured top left. Going clockwise is Catherine Blodgett, the first female scientist who invented non-reflecting glass (and we artists thank her), XRays and MRIS, turbines, an aging artifact (GE workers walked the "subway" going from Lower Broadway St. to work at the plant), harnessing wind energy and the future of robotics. The iconic 36 foot in diameter GE logo, colloquially called the "meatball", went atop Building 37 in 1926 and was the largest electrical sign in the country. It is lit by 1,399 light bulbs which change to red and green in December.

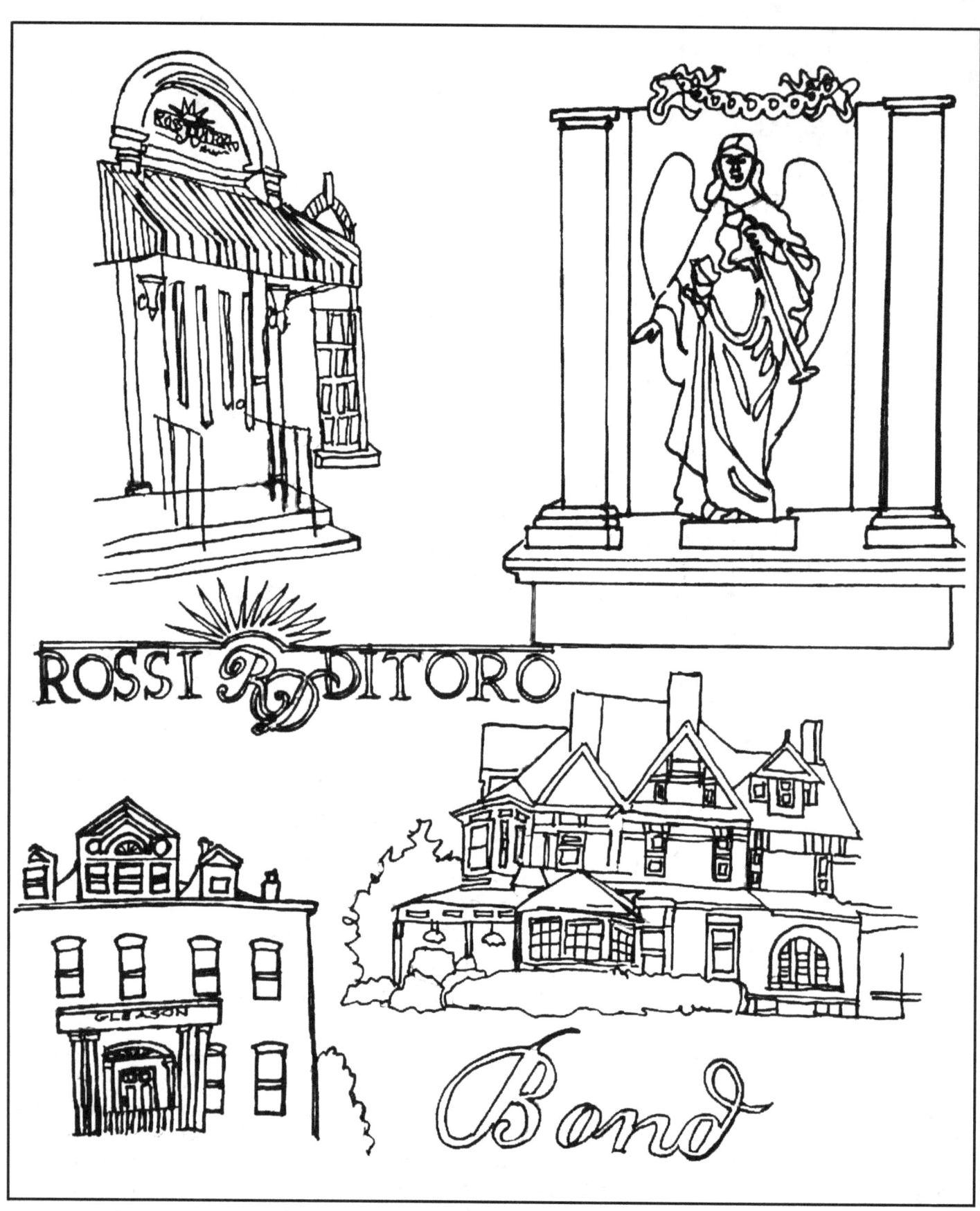

There are several old practitioners of the funereal business including Bonds and Rossi-Ditoro; however, Gleason is the oldest. Jim Gleason's great uncle opened its doors in 1890. Vale cemetery is represented here with an elegant statue. George Westinghouse built the Bond building for his mother in 1887 for his mother, but she declined, saying it was too big and too far away (from the Stockade)

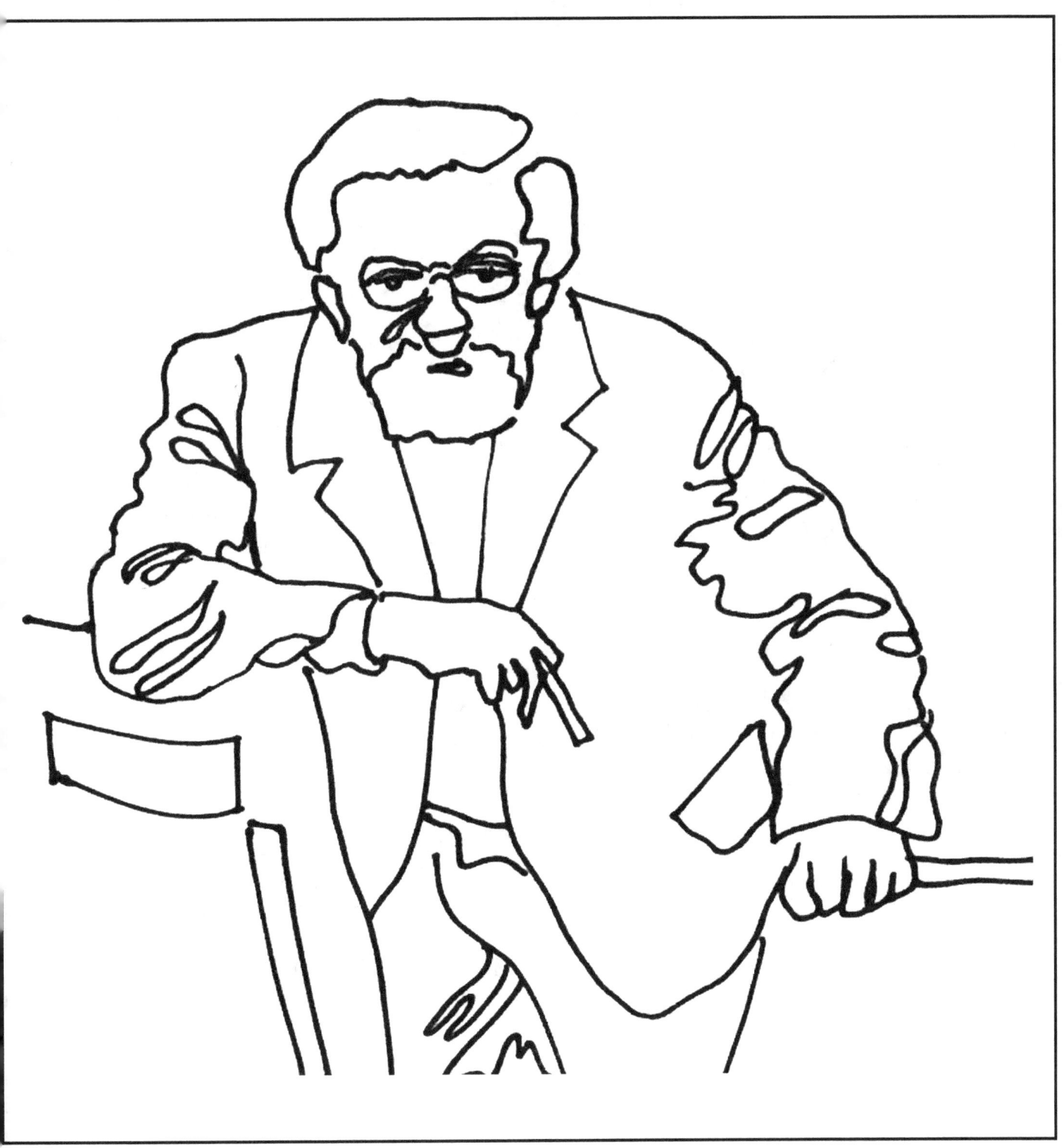

Charles Proteus Steinmetz was born in Prussia and lived from 1865-1923. He was the top electrical engineer in the U.S. and the "patron saint of the GE motor business". . He held over 200 patents. He lived in Schenectady on Wendell Ave. and his likeness appears on a stone sculpture on the foundation of his house there as well as talking with Edison on Erie Blvd. Steinmetz was a mathematician who taught electrical engineering at Union College but more importantly fostered the development of alternating currents that made possible the expansion of the electric power industry in the U.S. He made ground breaking discoveries in the understanding of hysteresis. (something to do with magnets). Although he suffered from dwarfism and hip dysphasia, his genius more than made up for it. He became known as the "Forger of Lightning Bolts" recreating lightning in the research lab at GE (the first research lab in the country). He kept pet rattlesnakes, black widow spiders and alligators, the latter of which kept escaping into the Erie Canal. I'm really glad I wasn't around to witness that.

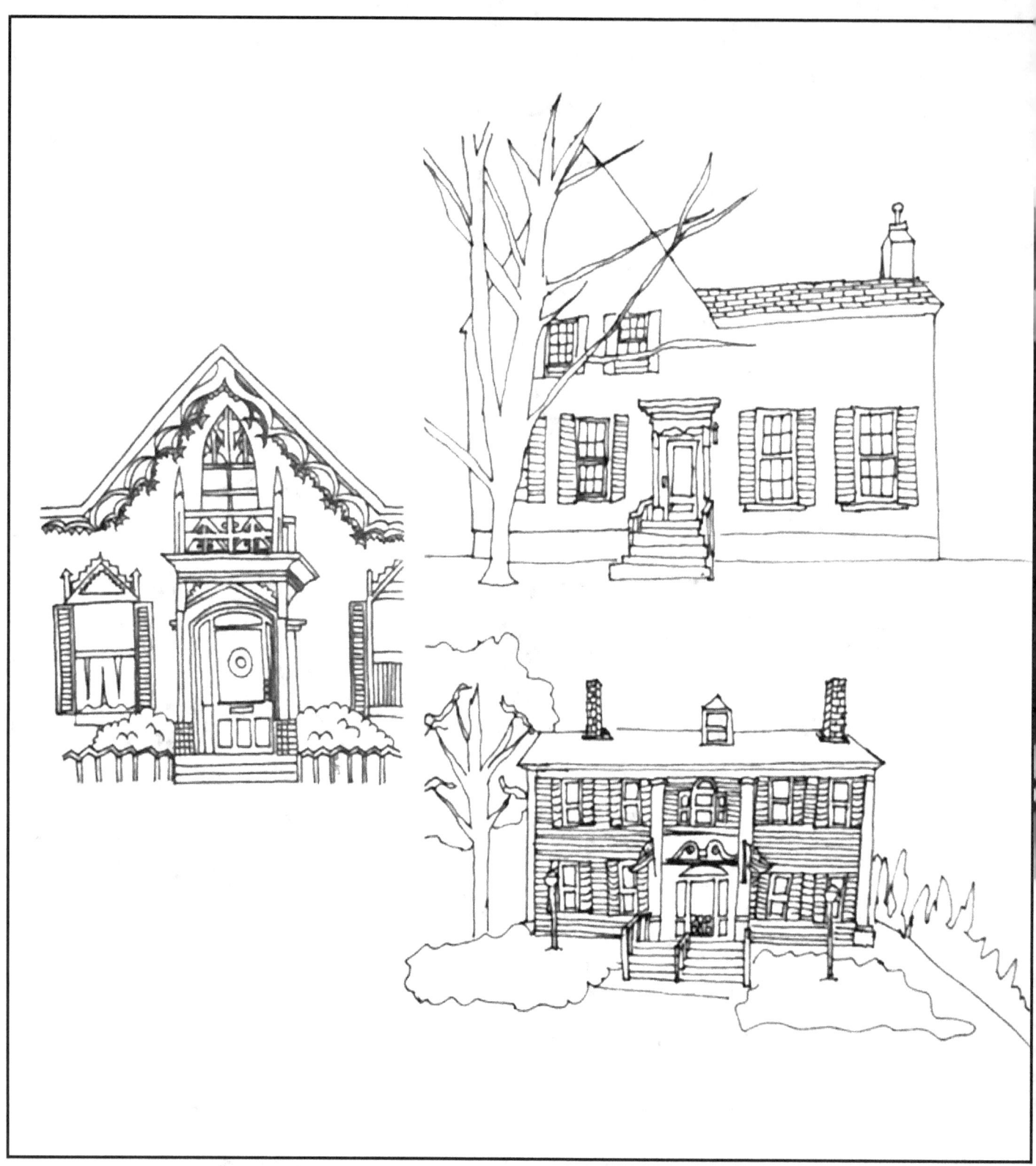

The Stockade Historic District is the largest collection of continuously inhabited 17th and 18th century homes in the country with over 40 homes over 200 years old. Settled in 1661, burned and resettled in 1692 with the help of Native Americans, here you will find original brick, cobblestone streets and architectural elements of the sturdy homes of local merchants, laborers and farmers of Dutch, English, and Scot heritage. It was a flourishing fur-trading outpost and a thriving industrial and commercial center. Clockwise from top, The Yates house has been argued to be the oldest of Dutch structures built in the US. The Schenectady Historical Society house is a fine example of Federal style. The last is an example of Gothic Revival style with "gingerbread" and other charming architectural elements.

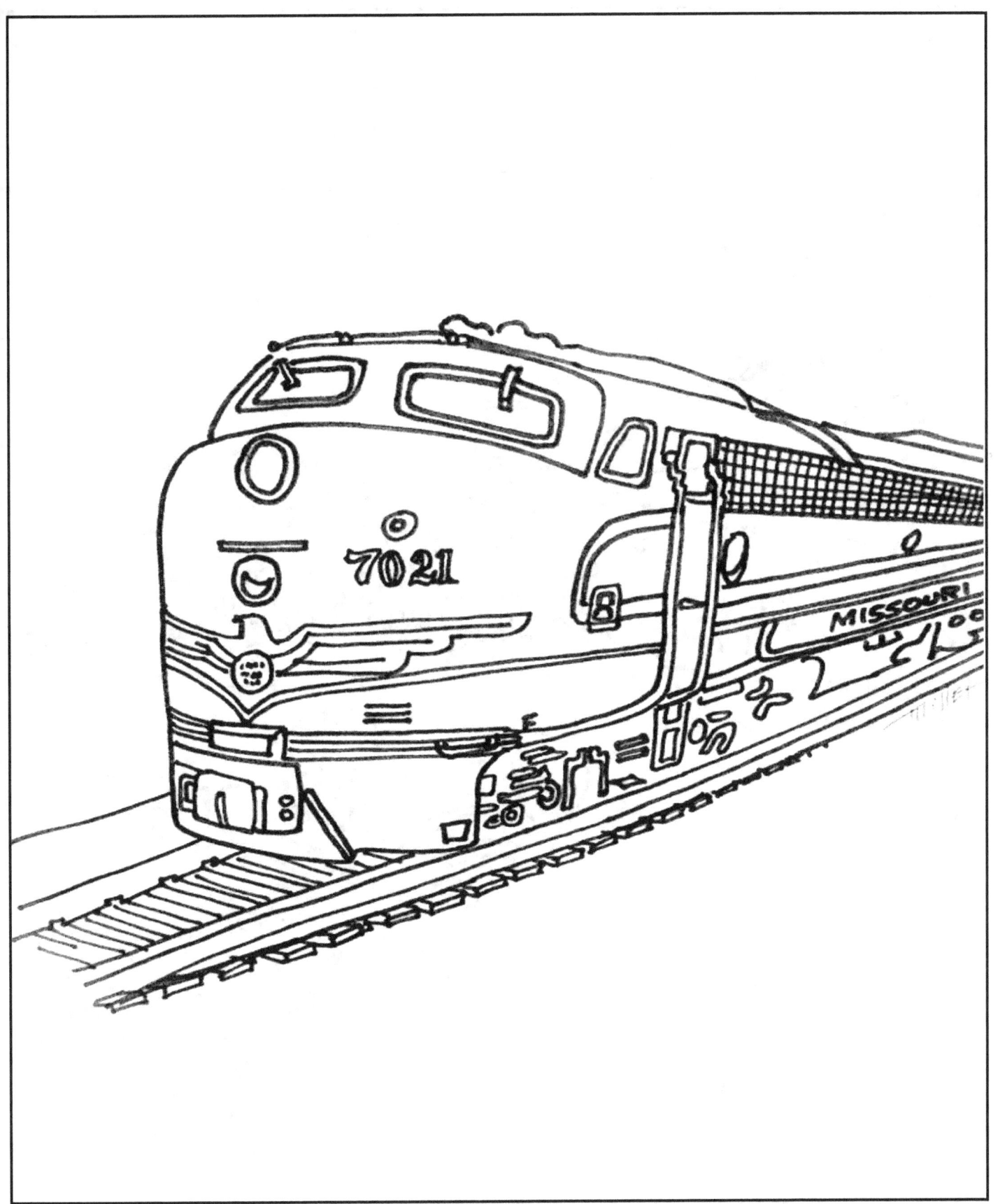

Alco, American Locomotive, set up shop in Schenectady from 1901-1969 and was the second largest manufacturer of locomotives in the U.S. They designed, built and sold locomotives, diesel engines, steel, tanks, automobiles and much more. Another Schenectady first is the advent of the Mohawk Hudson Railroad...one of the first passenger service trains in the U.S.

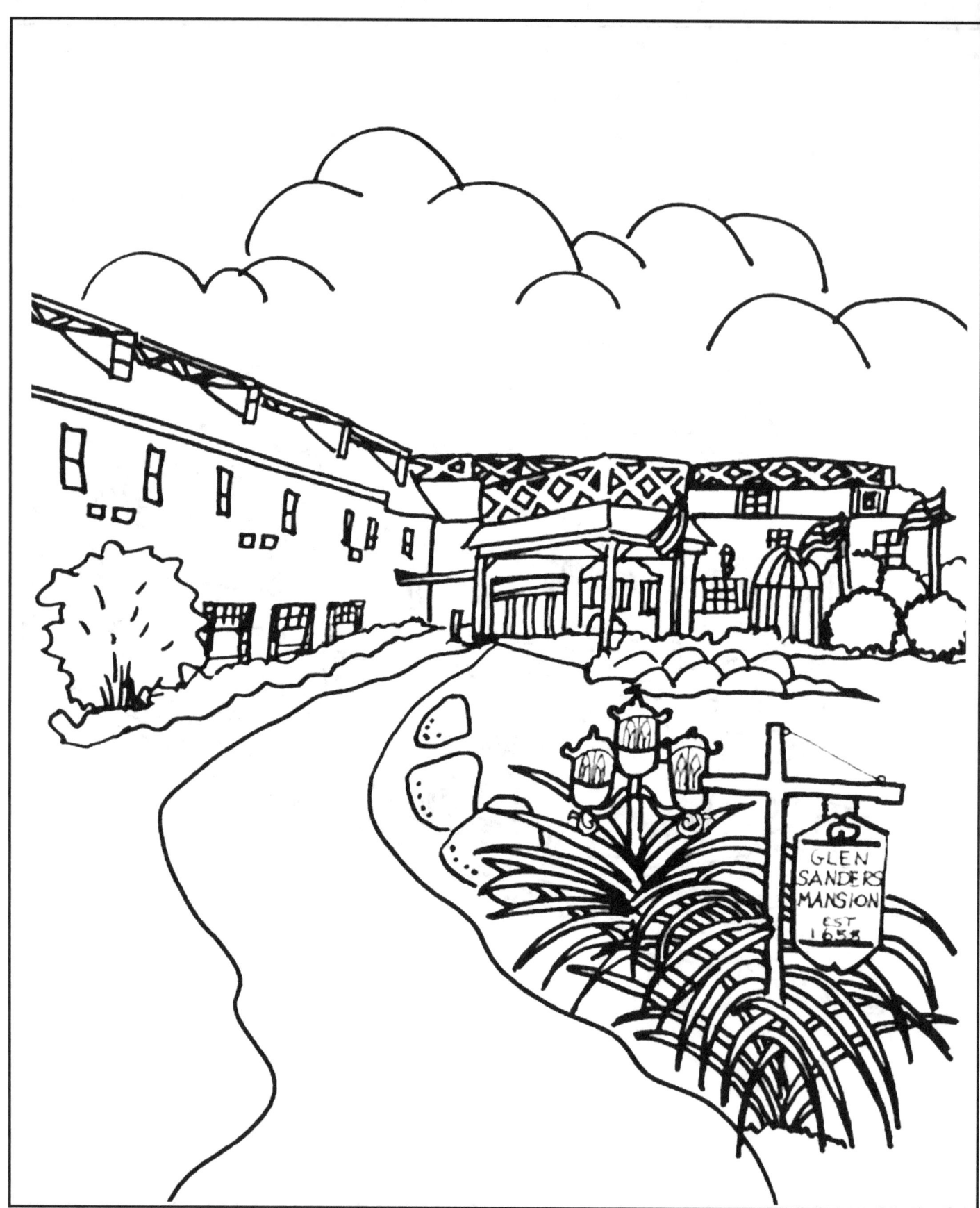

The Glen Sanders Mansion is not in Schenectady proper but across the Western Gateway Bridge in Scotia. I could not resist mentioning it because of its beauty and history. Founded in the 17th century, it was originally a trading port on the Mohawk and is named for two families integral to our history, the Glens and the Sanders. It is now a beautiful restaurant and Inn and hosts many events throughout the yet.

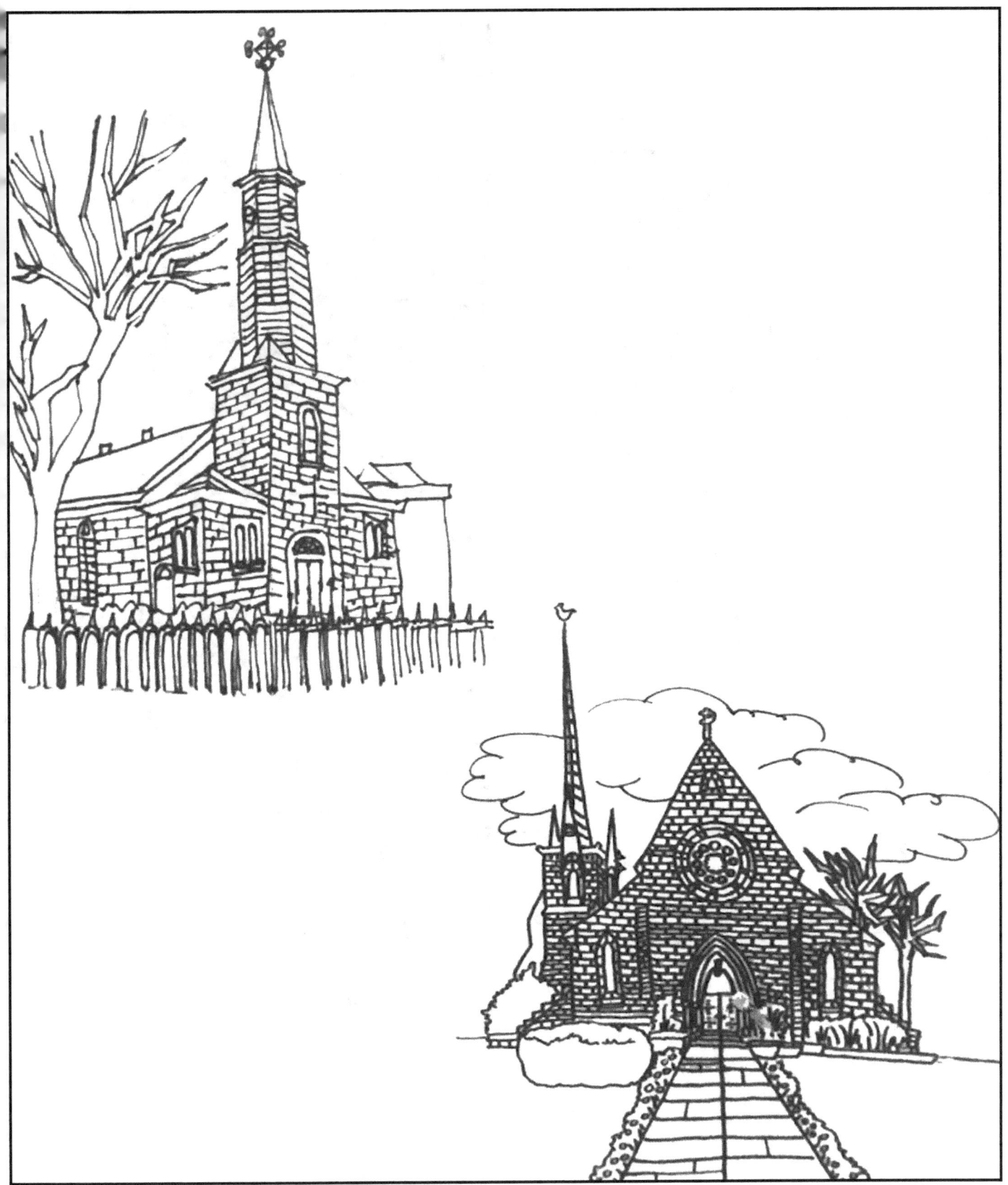

Although there are many beautiful churches, two of the oldest are in the Stockade Historic District. If you want a real feel for where our ancestors worshipped, visit St. Georges. It is an incredible piece of our history…it is the original bluestone building built in 1759 with its accompanying cemetery that houses graves dating from the 1700s. People have claimed to have seen ghosts here but I'd rather not find out.

Built in 1680, the First Reformed Church has gone through many changes. Now Its' elegant oak doors and Rose stained glass window are testaments to its endurance. Both churches' communicants included Native Americans.

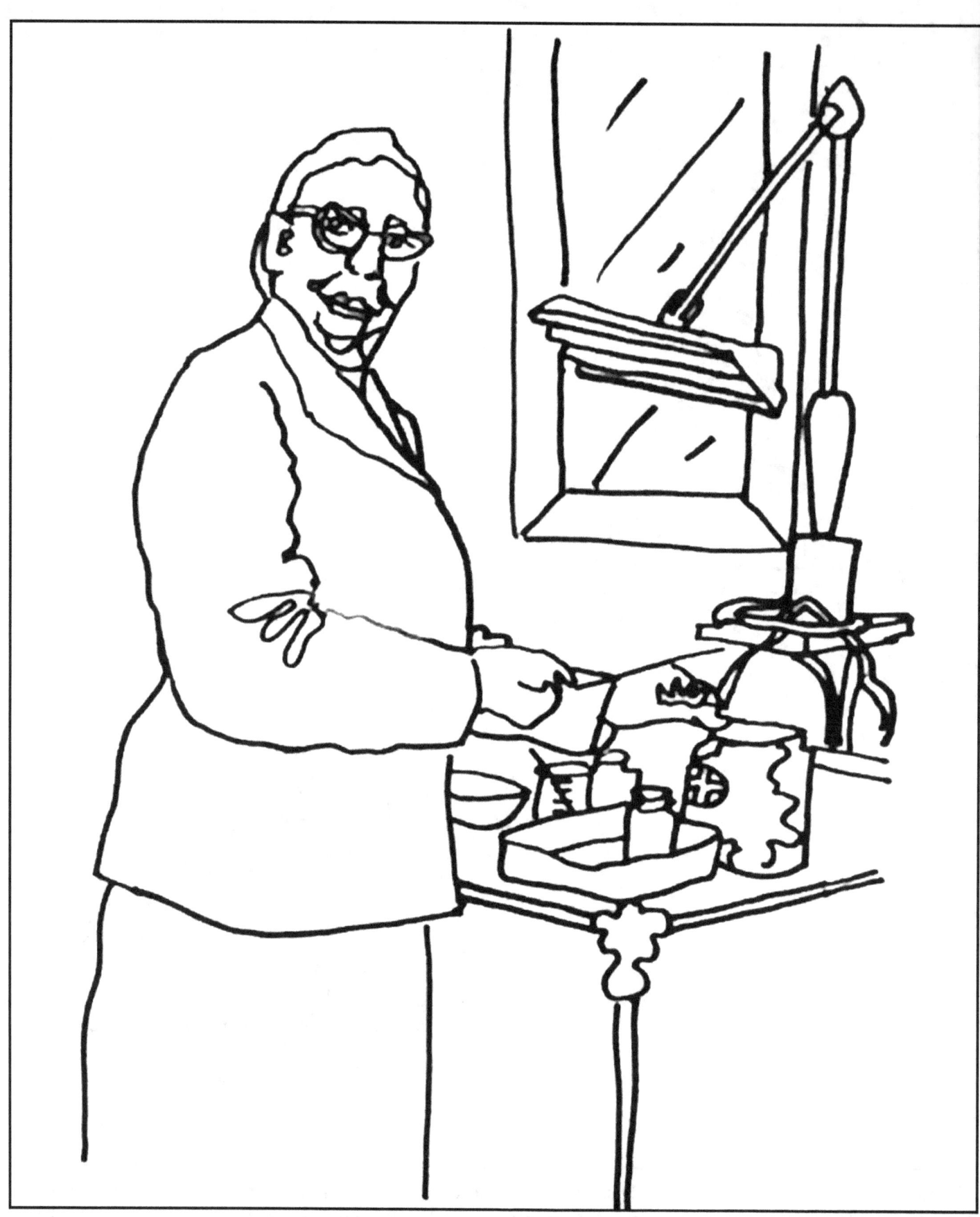

Dr. Elizabeth Gillette was the first female physician in Schenectady and is considered to be the first women surgeon in Schenectady County. She began her practice on June 1, 1900 and it lasted almost six decades. She retired in 1959 at age 85. Gillette lived and died in her home at the corner of Union and College Streets at the entrance to the Stockade.

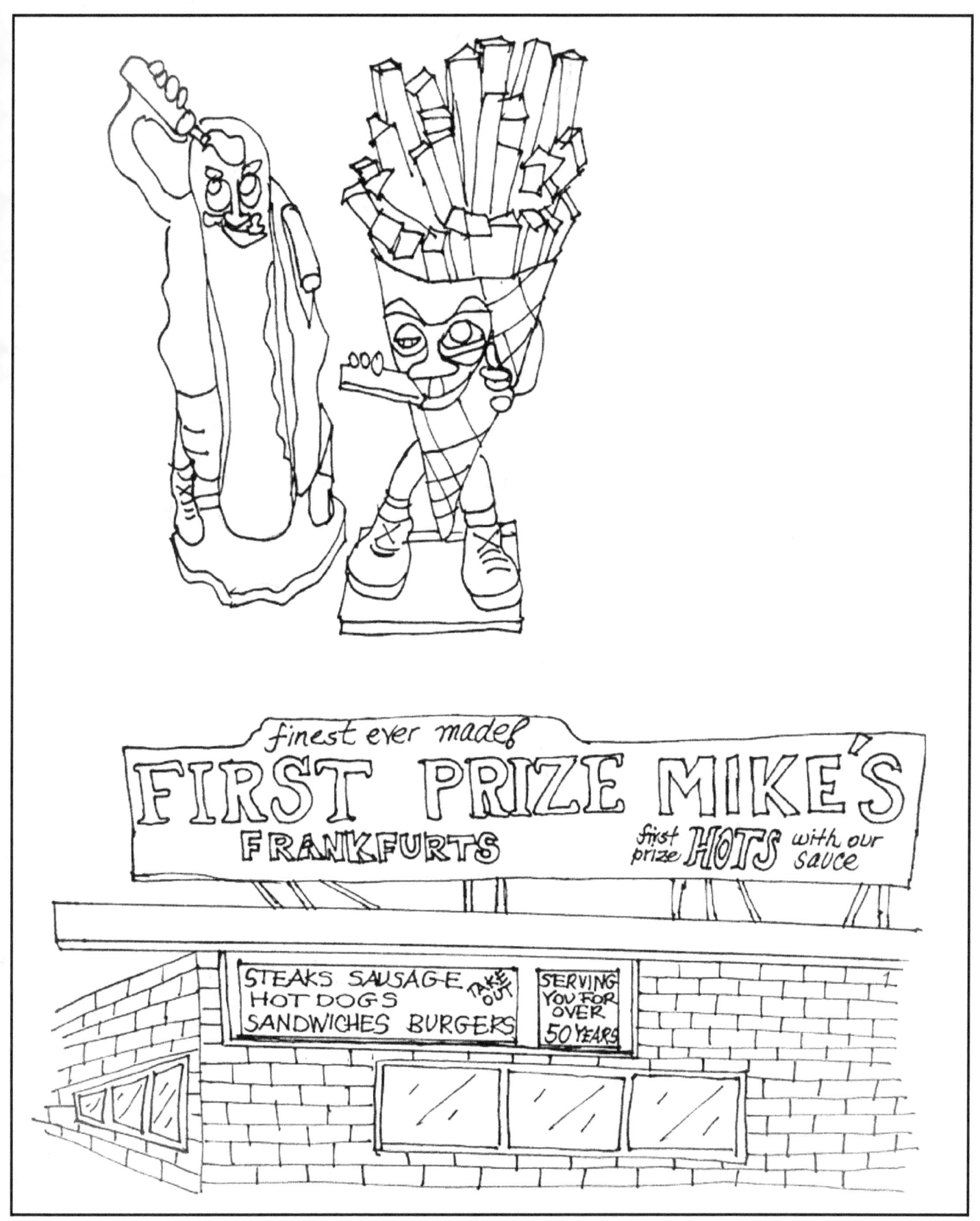

Mikes First Prize diner, opened in 1947, houses an original wooden phone booth and a feeling of an era long past. Stop here for their famous hot dogs and meat sauce or hearty breakfast. Take a selfie in front of the iconic hot dog and French Fry characters outside.

VIA
AQUARIUM